GARDEN CRAFTS

FLOWER, FRUIT & VEGETABLE CRAFT DESIGNS

Publications International, Ltd.

c r e d i t s

Craft Designers: Gerry Bauman/The Farmhouse (pages 46, 55); Lori Blankenship (pages 65, 142); Sue Carson (pages 114, 153); Pam Cowley (page 121); Gay Faye of Suzann Designs (pages 78, 85); Jill Fitzhenry (page 81); Judy Gibbs/Hollie Designs (pages 27, 159); Janelle Hayes (pages 102, 106, 111, 128, 162); Allan Howze (page 57); Janet Immordino (pages 33, 42, 100, 150, 165); Charlene Messerle (pages 24, 52, 62); Maria Nerius (pages 44, 74); Jan Patek/Jan Patek Quilts (page 130); Abby Ruoff (pages 30, 109, 135); Judith Sandstrom (page 38); Ann Snuggs (page 49); Muriel Spencer (pages 69, 87); Carol Spooner (pages 36, 94, 98, 117, 138, 145).

Technical Advisors: Carol L. Spooner, Karen Stolzenberg, Ann Wasserman, Pamela A. Zimny

Photography: Peter Dean Ross Photographs, Sacco Productions Limited/Chicago, IL

Photo Credits: Photo/Nats, Inc.: Gay Bumgarner: 22-23, 60-61, 96-97, David M. Stone: 126-127.

Photo Stylists: Sally Grimes, Hilary Rose/With Style, Melissa J. Sacco, Paula M. Walters

Models: Karen Edwards and Theresa Lesniak/Royal Model Management

Photo Sites: Leslee Cerventes, T. R. Leach, Wanda McDonald, Teresa and Walter Moeller, Dina Petrakis, Ann Ralston, Carol Szalacha, Cotswolds on the Lake Development, Northbrook, IL

Location Scouts: Dana Cleary, Sally Mauer/With Style

Floral Acknowledgements: Flowerfields & Co., Schaumburg, IL; Platz Fresh Flower Wholesaler, Morton Grove, IL; Red River Vine Co., Texarkana, TX; Tom Thumb Workshop, Mappsville, VA

Louis Weber, C.E.O.
Publications International, Ltd.
7373 North Cicero Avenue
Lincolnwood, Illinois 60646

Permission is never granted for commercial purposes.

Manufactured in USA.

8 7 6 5 4 3 2 1

ISBN: 0-7853-1295-1

Library of Congress Catalog Card Number: 95-72540

contents

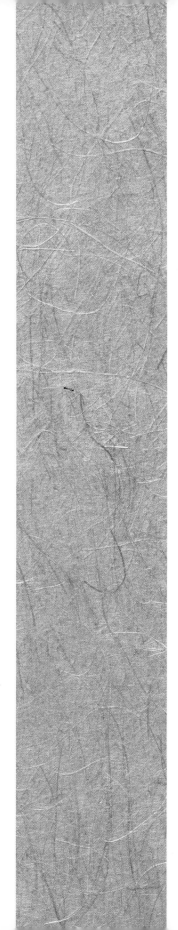

garden party

at home in the garden

sources for products • *167*

index • *168*

i n t r o d u c t i o n

The projects in this book include a wide variety of techniques and methods. You'll find everything from traditional crafts to today's new materials and techniques. We've included projects for all skill levels. Each one has complete step-by-step instructions and photos to help make everything easy to understand and fun to do. However, the basic information that follows will help you get started.

Before plunging into your chosen project, read the directions thoroughly. Check to make sure you have all the materials needed. Being prepared will make your project easier and more enjoyable. Many of the items you need may be on hand already. Your local craft store will be a good source of materials.

Next, read the basic information in the pages that follow for the craft you're doing. These pages will define terms, help you choose materials, and describe certain techniques that are essential to that craft.

USING PATTERNS

Enlarging patterns: Many of the patterns in this book are printed smaller than actual size in order to fit them on the page. You will have to enlarge them before starting the project. You can do this on a photocopier, copying the pattern at the percentage indicated. If you don't have access to a photocopier, you can use the grid method.

You will need graph paper or other paper ruled in one-inch squares. The first step is to draw a grid of evenly spaced lines over the pattern in the book. (You will probably want to trace the pattern and draw the grid over the tracing rather than drawing directly in the book.) The next step is to copy, square by square, the pattern from the smaller grid in the book to the one-inch graph paper. Using the grid ensures that the pattern is enlarged proportionately.

The size of the grid you draw on the pattern depends on the degree of enlargement you need. If the pattern is to be 200 percent of what is in the book, your grid will consist of half-inch squares. If the pattern is to be copied at 150 percent, the squares in your grid will be two-thirds of an inch.

Transferring patterns: Once your pattern is the correct size, you can use it as directed in the project instructions. One method is to transfer a pattern to another surface by tracing over the lines of the pattern with an iron-on transfer pen. Follow the manufacturer's directions to iron the pattern onto the surface. You can also use transfer paper. Sandwich the transfer paper between the pattern and the surface.

A WORD ABOUT GLUE

Glue can be a sticky subject when you don't use the right one for the job. Many different glues are on the craft market today, each formulated for a different crafting purpose. The following are ones you should be familiar with.

White glue: This may be used as an all-purpose glue—it dries clear and flexible. It is often referred to as craft glue or tacky glue. Tacky on contact, it allows you to put two items together without a lot of set-up time. Use for most projects, especially wood, plastics, some fabrics, and cardboard.

Thin-bodied glues: Use these glues when your project requires a smooth, thin layer of glue. Thin-bodied glues work well on some fabrics and papers.

Hot-melt glue: Formed into cylindrical sticks, this glue is inserted into a hot-temperature glue gun and heated to a liquid state. Depending on the type of glue gun used, the glue is forced out through the gun's nozzle by either pushing on the end of the glue stick or squeezing a trigger. Use clear glue sticks for projects using wood, fabrics, most plastics, ceramics, and cardboard. When using any glue gun, be careful of the nozzle and the freshly applied glue—it is very hot! Apply glue to the piece being attached. Work with small areas at a time so that the glue doesn't set before being pressed into place.

Low-melt glue: Like hot-melt glue, low-melt glue is formed into sticks and requires a glue gun to be used. Low-melt glues are used for projects that would be damaged by heat. Examples include foam, balloons, and metallic ribbons. Low-melt glue sticks are oval-shaped and can be used only in a cool-temperature glue gun.

DECORATIVE PAINTING

Decorative painting is an art form that was developed by untrained artists—no artistic talent or drawing skills are necessary. All you need is the desire to create useful and beautiful items to decorate your home.

paints and supplies

Paints: Acrylic paint dries in minutes, and cleanup is easy with soap and water. Many brands of acrylic paints are available at your local arts and crafts stores. The projects in this book will work with any brand, so you can choose your favorite colors regardless of brand.

Finishes: Varnishes to protect your finished project are available in both spray or brush-on. Brush-on water-base varnish dries in minutes and cleans up with soap and water. Use it over any acrylic paints. Spray varnish can be used over any type of paint or medium. For projects with a pure white surface, choose a nonyellowing varnish. The slight yellowing of some varnishes can actually enhance certain colors for a richer look. Varnishes are available in matte, satin, or gloss finishes. Choose the shine you prefer.

brushes

Foam (sponge) brushes work well for sealing, basecoating, and varnishing wood. They can be cleaned with soap and water when using acrylic paints and mediums, but for paints or mediums that require mineral spirits to clean up, you will have to throw the disposable brush away.

Synthetic brushes work well with acrylic paints for details and designs. You will use a liner brush for thin lines and details. Round brushes fill in round areas and are used for stroke work and broad lines. An angle brush is used to fill in large areas and to float, or side-load, color. A large flat brush is used to apply basecoat and varnish. Small flat brushes are for stroke work and basecoating small areas. Specialty brushes, including a stencil brush and a fabric round scrubber, can be used for stencil painting.

wood preparation

Properly preparing your wood piece so it has a smooth surface to work on is important to the success of your project. Once the wood is prepared, you are ready to proceed with a basecoat, stain, or finish.

Supplies you will need to prepare the wood: sandpaper (#200) for removing roughness; tack cloth, which is a sticky, resin-treated cheesecloth to remove dust after sanding; a wood sealer to seal wood and prevent warping; and a foam or 1-inch flat brush to apply sealer.

basic painting techniques

Thin lines

1. Thin paint with 50 percent water for a fluid consistency that flows easily off the brush. It should be about ink consistency.

2. Use a liner brush for short lines and tiny details or a script brush for long lines. Dip brush into thinned paint. Wipe excess on palette.

3. Hold brush upright with handle pointing to the ceiling. Use your little finger as a balance when painting. Don't apply pressure for extra thin lines.

Floating color

This technique is also called side-loading. It is used to shade or highlight the edge of an object. Floated color is a gradual blend of color to water.

1. Moisten an angle brush with water. Blot excess water from brush, setting bristles on paper towel until shine of water disappears.

2. Dip the long corner of the angle brush into paint. Load paint sparingly. Carefully stroke the brush on your palette until the color blends halfway across the brush. If the paint blends all the way to the short side, clean the brush and load again. Dilute thicker paint first with 50 percent water.

3. Hold the brush at a 45 degree angle and, using a light touch, apply color to designated area.

Stenciling

A stencil is a design or shape cut out of a sheet of thin, strong plastic. You can paint perfect designs by simply applying paint inside the shape with a stencil brush. A sponge or old brush with bristles cut short will also work.

1. Use a precut stencil pattern or make your own by drawing a design on a sheet of plastic and cutting it out with a craft knife. Tape the stencil onto the surface you are painting.

2. Don't thin the paint. Dip the tip of a stencil brush in the paint color. Blot almost all paint off on paper towel. Too much paint or watery paint can bleed under the stencil and cause uneven edges. Practice on paper first.

3. Hold the brush in an upright position and pounce repeatedly inside the cutout area. Make color heavy on the edges and sparse in the center for a shaded look.

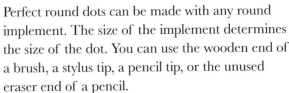

Dots

Perfect round dots can be made with any round implement. The size of the implement determines the size of the dot. You can use the wooden end of a brush, a stylus tip, a pencil tip, or the unused eraser end of a pencil.

1. Use undiluted paint for thick dots or dilute paint with 50 percent water for smooth dots. Dip the tip into paint and then place the tip on the surface. For uniform dots, you must redip in paint for each dot. For graduated dots, continue dotting with same paint load. Clean tip on paper towel after each group and reload.

RUBBER STAMPS

With rubber stamps, you can create your own greeting cards, stationery, wrapping paper, fabric designs—even jewelry! All you need to start are a few stamps, ink pads, papers, and accessories.

supplies

Stamps: The variety of images available in rubber stamps is enormous. Most rubber-stamp projects use a number of stamps to create a unique picture.

Inks: The standard, dye-based ink used in some ink pads is water-based. Never use permanent inks for a rubber-stamp project; they will ruin your stamps. Dye-based inks are easy to use, and the ink dries quickly. This type of ink pad is sold everywhere and comes in dozens of colors.

Pigment ink is thick, opaque, and slow-drying— not good for slick surfaces, but perfect for embossing. Pigment ink also works well when stamping on colored paper, because the color of the paper won't show through or alter the color of the overlying ink. For stamping in metallic colors, pigment inks are unequalled.

Papers: Suitable types of paper for stamping have smooth surfaces and are white or light-colored. Dark or textured paper is suitable only in rare cases—for example, when stamped with metallic ink and embossed. Glossy, matte, and coated stock come in a range of colors and weights. Some work better with dye-based ink; others work better with pigment ink.

Tools: Rubber-stamp projects use many of the following items: colored pencils, water-based brush markers, embossing powders and embossing gun, glitter glue, scissors, pinking shears, glue gun, craft knives and cutting mat, brayer, fabric ink and marking pens, eraser carving material and carving tools, stamp positioning tool, and cosmetic sponges.

techniques

No matter what stamping project you've chosen, you need to understand the basics before you begin. Keep these tips in mind:

1. Know the fundamental stamping variables. The stamp, ink, and paper are most important, and each affects the other. Experiment every time you get a new stamp to see how it takes ink and leaves an impression. Check out its resiliency, and observe how it stamps on different papers or surfaces. Test new ink pads and papers as well.

2. Learn the correct way to ink a stamp. Tap the stamp gently two or three times on a pad. Never pound or rock a stamp when inking. Turn the stamp over to see how well it's inked. Stamp it on scrap paper to get a feel for applying the right amount of ink to a stamp. Too little ink causes details to be lost and colors to look pale, whereas too much ink obscures details. The image on a new stamp usually needs heavier inking because the fresh surface is so porous.

3. Perfect your general stamping technique. Make a stamp impression by gently and evenly applying the inked stamp to the paper. Do not grind or rock the stamp.

4. Always work with clean stamps. Clean off each stamp before you switch from one color to another and after you are finished using it. Prepare a cleaning plate by moistening a paper towel, sponge, or small rag under warm running water, then wringing it out. Place it on a water-proof plate or in a shallow bowl. After using a stamp, tap it several times on scrap paper to remove as much ink as possible, then tap it onto the cleaning plate. Finally, tap it onto a clean paper towel or rag to remove moisture. Never use alcohol-based solvents or other harsh cleansing agents—they can ruin a stamp.

5. Protect your stamps when they're not in use. Store with the die side down, out of direct sunlight and away from dust. Line your stamp storage container with thick construction paper.

Inking and coloring stamps: You can ink a stamp in several ways. The easiest is to tap it onto a pad. Another way is to ink with a felt-tip marker.

This method lets you color various parts of an image in different hues. To do this, hold your stamp in one hand with the die facing you, and color it directly with one or more markers. Work swiftly to keep the ink from drying out. When done, breathe gently on the stamp for more moisture, then stamp.

Masking: Masking lets you add one image to another in a clever way. For practice, select an image

to which you'd like to attach part of a second image. Stamp the base image on a sticky note so that some of the note's adhesive edge will remain after cutting out the image. This is your mask. Next, stamp the same image on a sheet of paper. Stick the cut-out mask on top of it. Stamp the same or a different image over the masked image so that part of it prints on the paper, part on the mask.

Remove the mask.

CROSS-STITCH

Cross-stitch is traditionally worked on an even-weave cloth that has vertical and horizontal threads of equal thickness and spacing. The cloth can have as few as five threads to the inch or as many as 22. The most common even-weave fabric is 14-count Aida cloth, meaning it has 14 threads to the inch. Designs can be stitched on any fabric count—the resulting size of the project is the only thing that will be affected. Since the count number refers to the number of stitches per inch, the smaller the count number of the fabric, the larger

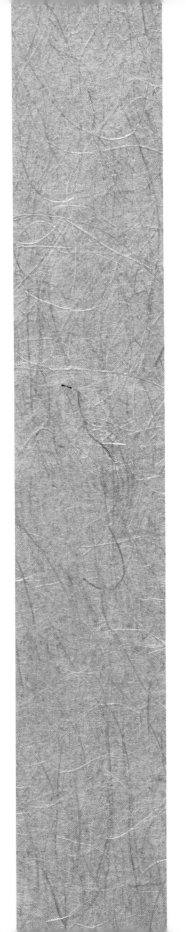

the design will be. Thus a design worked on 14-count fabric will be half the size of the same design worked on 7-count fabric. Most of the projects in this book are worked on prefinished products that include even-weave cloth for cross-stitching.

Six-strand embroidery floss is used for most stitching. Many other beautiful threads, particularly metallic threads, can be used to enhance the appearance of the stitching.

basic supplies

Needles, hoops, and scissors: A blunt-end or tapestry needle is used for counted cross-stitch. The recommended size for most stitching is a #24 needle. You can use an embroidery hoop while stitching—just be sure to remove it when not working on your project. A small pair of sharp scissors is a definite help when working with embroidery floss.

Floss: Six-strand cotton embroidery floss is most commonly used, and it's usually cut into 18-inch lengths for stitching. Use two of the six strands unless the directions for that project tell you otherwise. Also use two strands for backstitching, unless the directions state otherwise.

preparing to stitch

Directions for the cross-stitch projects in this book will tell you the size of the piece of cloth you need to complete the project.

Position the center of the design in the center of the fabric. To locate the center of the fabric, lightly fold it in half and in half again. Find the center of the chart by following the arrows on the side and top.

Reading the chart is easy—each square on the chart equals one stitch on the fabric. Near each chart you will find a color key listing the colors used and showing a representative square of each color. Select a color and stitch all of that color within an area. Begin by holding the thread ends behind the fabric until secured or covered over with two or three stitches. You can skip a few stitches on the back of the material to get from one area to another, but do not run the thread behind a section that will not be stitched in the finished piece—it will show through the fabric.

If your thread begins to twist, drop the needle and allow the thread to untwist. It is important to the final appearance of the project to keep an even tension when pulling stitches through so that all stitches will have a uniform look. To end a thread, weave or run the thread under several stitches on the back side. Cut the ends close to the fabric.

Horizontal rows:
Cross all stitches in the same direction. Work the stitches in two steps—first do all the left-to-right stitches (bringing your needle up at 1 and down at 2), and then go back over them to do all the right-to-left stitches (bringing your needle up at 3 and down at 4).

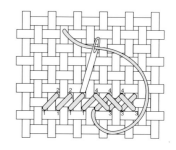

Vertical rows:

Work each complete stitch before going on to the next, bringing your needle up at 1, down at 2, up at 3, and down at 4.

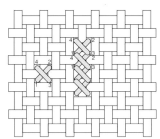

Backstitch:

Outlining and creating letters is often done in backstitch, which is shown by bold lines on the patterns. Your needle comes up at 1 and all odd-numbered holes and goes down at 2 and all even-numbered holes. Backstitch is usually worked after the pattern is completed.

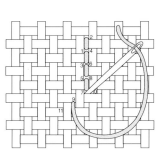

PLASTIC CANVAS

Plastic canvas allows for three-dimensional stitchery projects to be constructed. Stitching on plastic canvas is easy to do, easy on the eyes, and easy on the pocketbook, too.

basic supplies

Plastic canvas: Canvas is most widely available by the sheet. Stitch all the pieces of a project on the same brand of plastic canvas to ensure that the meshes will match if you need to join them together.

Plastic canvas comes in several counts, or mesh sizes (number of stitches to the inch), just as cross-stitch fabric does. Specialty sizes and shapes such as circles are also available. Most canvas is clear, although up to 24 colors are available. Colored canvas is used when parts of the project remain unstitched. Seven-count canvas comes in four weights—standard; a thinner, flexible weight; a stiffer, rigid weight; and a softer weight made especially for bending and curved projects.

Needles: Needle size is determined by the count size of the plastic canvas you are using. Patterns generally call for a #18 needle for stitching on 7-count plastic canvas, a #16 or #18 for 10-count plastic canvas, and a #22 or #24 for stitching on 14-count plastic canvas.

Yarns: A wide variety of yarns can be used. The most common is worsted weight, or 4-ply, yarn. Wool yarn can be used, but acrylic yarns are less expensive and also are washable. Several companies produce specialty yarns for plastic canvas work. These cover the canvas well and will not "pill" as some acrylics do. Sport-weight, or 3-ply, yarn and embroidery floss are often used on 10-count canvas. Use 6 strands of embroidery floss for stitching on 14-count canvas and 12 strands, or double the floss thickness, for 10-count canvas. Many of the specialty metallic threads made for cross-stitch can be used to highlight and enhance your project.

preparing to stitch

Cut your yarn to a 36-inch length. Begin by holding the yarn end behind the fabric until secured or

covered over with two or three stitches. To end a length, weave or run the yarn under several stitches on the back side. Cut the end close to the canvas.

As in cross-stitch, if your yarn begins to twist, drop the needle and allow the yarn to untwist. It is important to the final appearance of the project to keep an even tension when pulling your stitches through so that all your stitches have a uniform look. Do not pull your stitches too tight, since this causes gaps in your stitching and allows the canvas to show through between your stitches. Also do not carry one color of yarn across too many rows of another color on the back—the carried color may show through to the front of your project.

Do not stitch the outer edge of the canvas until the other stitching is complete. If the project is a single piece of canvas, overcast the outer edge with the color specified. If two or more pieces are used, follow the pattern instructions for assembly.

Beading: You will use thread rather than yarn to bead. The stitch is the same as the continental stitch (see next column) except you add a bead for each stitch. The stitch chart for the project will show the continental stitch but on the finished project, the beads will angle the opposite direction.

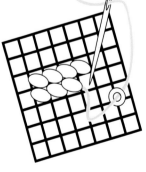

Continental stitch: This is the most commonly used stitch to cover plastic canvas. Bring your needle up at 1 and all odd-numbered holes and down at 2 and all even-numbered holes.

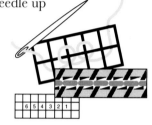

Backstitch: For the backstitch, the needle comes up at 1 and down at the square to the right. Then bring the needle up at 2 and down at the square to the right. Continue on with each numbered hole with the needle coming up and going down at the square to the right.

cleaning your project

Projects stitched with acrylic yarn can be washed by hand using warm or cool water and a mild detergent. Place the item on a terry-cloth towel to air dry. Don't dry-clean plastic canvas or dry it in a dryer.

RIBBON EMBROIDERY

Ribbon embroidery is much like regular embroidery or crewel work, except you use silk or silklike ribbon instead of yarn or floss. Be careful to keep ribbon untwisted as you work and you will work much looser stitches than in traditional embroidery. A few practice stitches will show you how easy embroidery with ribbon really is!

Cut ribbon lengths into 12- to 14-inch lengths, angle-cutting the ends of the ribbon. Thread the ribbon through the eye of the needle and, about ½ inch from one end, pierce through the center of the ribbon with the needle. Pull other end of ribbon until the ribbon "locks" into place. To begin stitching, make a knot at the end of the ribbon and trim tail close to knot. To finish stitching, either tie off ribbon next to the fabric or make a few small backstitches and trim tail. If you plan on washing your finished project, use a drop of washable glue to keep ribbon from fraying.

Stem stitch: Bring needle up at A, down at B, and up at C. Continue this stitch, making sure to space stitches evenly.

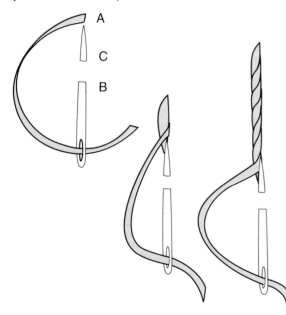

French knot:
Bring needle up and wrap ribbon around needle once. Insert needle right next to insertion point and put your finger on ribbon as you slowly pull ribbon through.

 Freeform rose: The center is a French knot and straight stitches are filled in around the knot.

SEWING

Before starting a sewing project, read through the directions and study the photographs to make sure you understand how the project is put together.

materials

Fabrics: The type of fabric best suited to the project is given in the list of materials. But don't hesitate to make substitutions, taking into consideration your preferences in colors and patterns. Keep in mind the scale of a pattern relative to the size of the project. The weight of the fabric is an important consideration: Don't substitute a heavy, stiff fabric for a delicate fabric.

It is worth investing in the best materials you can afford. Many inexpensive fabrics are less likely to be colorfast. Avoid the regret that goes with

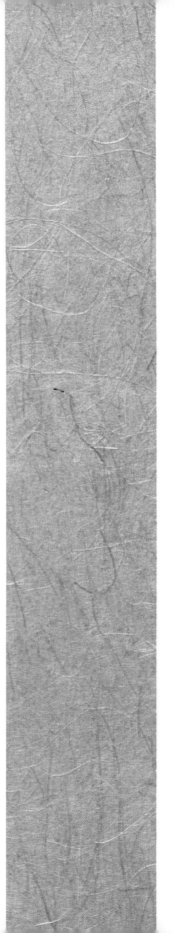

choosing a fabric that isn't quite perfect and is less expensive than the fabric you really love.

Thread: Have mercerized sewing thread in the colors needed for the project you have chosen. Using the proper shade and strength (about a 50 weight) of thread avoids having the stitching show more than is necessary, and the item will have a finished look.

Fusible webbing (or adhesive): This light-weight fusible iron-on adhesive makes easy work of attaching fabric cutouts to your garment. The webbing is placed paper side up on the wrong side of the material. Place the iron on the paper side of the adhesive and press for one to three seconds. Allow the fabric to cool. Your design can then be drawn or traced onto the paper side and cut out. To transfer patterns to fusible webbing, place pattern piece right side down on the paper backing. Trace around the pattern piece and cut out. Remove the paper and place the material right side up in the desired position on your project and iron for three to five seconds. If desired, you may machine-stitch a zigzag stitch around the attached fusible adhesive pieces to secure the edges.

t o o l s

Scissors: For cutting fabric, you'll need sharp scissors eight to ten inches long with a bent handle. This style of scissors allows you to cut through the fabric while the fabric lies flat. These scissor should be used only for fabric: paper and plastic quickly dull the cutting edges of scissors. You'll also need a smaller pair of scissors, about six inches, with sharp points, for smaller projects.

Straight pins: Nonrusting dressmaker pins will not leave rust marks on your fabric if they come in contact with dampness or glue. And dressmaker's pins have very sharp points.

Ironing board and steam iron: The iron is just as important to a sewing project as the sewing machine. Keeping your fabrics, seams, and hems pressed saves valuable time and produces a professional look. You also use the iron to adhere fusible interfacing. Be sure your ironing board is well padded and has a clean covering. Keep the bottom of your iron clean and free of any substance that could mark your fabric.

A steam-or-dry iron is best. The steam iron may be used directly on most fabrics with no shine. Test a small piece of the fabric first. If it causes a shine on the right side, try the reverse side.

Cutting out patterns: Some of the patterns in this book are smaller than actual size in order to fit them on the page. Instructions for enlarging patterns are on page 6. Many pattern pieces indicate that two pieces should be cut from the pattern. Fold the fabric in half, right sides together, lengthwise with the salvages together. Adjust one side to the left or right until the fabric hangs straight. The line created by the fold is parallel to the fabric's straight of grain. Place the pattern pieces right side up on the fabric with the arrow on the pattern lying along the grain line. On a pattern piece, a solid line indicates a cutting line, and a dashed line indicates a line that should be placed on the fold. To make sure you have enough fabric, arrange and pin all pattern pieces on the fabric before you start to cut.

QUILTING

Modern time-saving techniques for quilting allow even the busiest person to make quilts that can be used on beds or hung on a wall.

material selection

Fabric: The considerations for selecting fabrics for sewing projects apply to quilting as well. Try to select only 100 percent cotton fabrics for the face and back of the quilt. Cotton is easy to cut, mark, sew, and press. It is also widely available. Fabrics that contain synthetics, such as polyester, are more difficult to handle and are more likely to pucker.

The backing fabric should be similar in fiber content and care instructions to the fabrics used in the quilt top. Some wide cottons (90 and 108 inches) are sold specifically for quilt backings. They eliminate the need to piece the back.

Batting: Many types of batting are available to meet the needs of different projects. In general, use polyester batting with a low or medium loft. Polyester is better if the quilt will be washed frequently. All-cotton batting is preferred by some quilters for a very flat, traditional-looking quilt. For a puffier quilt, you can use a high-loft batting, but it is difficult to quilt.

Thread: Old, weak thread tangles and knots, making it frustrating to work with. Buy 100 percent cotton thread or good long-staple polyester thread for piecing, appliqué, and machine quilting. Cotton quilting thread is wonderful for hand quilting, but should not be used for machine quilt-ing because it is stiff and will tend to lie on the surface of the quilt.

For piecing by hand or by machine, select a neutral color of thread that blends in with most of the fabrics in the quilt. For most projects, either khaki or gray thread works well. Use white thread for basting; do not risk using colored thread, which could leave color behind. For appliqué, the thread should match the fabric that is being applied to the background. The color of quilting thread is a personal design choice. If you want your quilting to show up, use a contrasting color of thread.

material preparation

Prewashing: Always wash fabrics first. This will remove some of the chemicals added by the manufacturer, making it easier to quilt. Also, cotton fabric does shrink, and most of the shrinkage will occur during the first washing and drying. Be sure to use settings that are as hot as those you intend to use with the finished quilt.

Dark, intense colors, especially reds, tend to bleed or run. Wash these fabrics by themselves. If the water becomes colored, try soaking the fabric in a solution of three parts cold water to one part white wine vinegar. Rinse thoroughly. Wash again. If the fabric is still losing its color, discard the fabric and select another. It is not worth using a fabric that may ruin the other fabrics when the finished quilt is washed.

Marking and cutting fabric: Some of the patterns in this book are smaller than actual size in order to fit them on the page. Instructions for en-

larging patterns are on page 6. To cut fabric the traditional way for piecing or appliqué, place the pattern right side down on the wrong side of the fabric.

Trace around the pattern with a hard-lead pencil or a colored pencil designed for marking on fabric. Cut around each piece with sharp fabric scissors.

In many cases, it is faster and easier to cut fabric using a rotary cutter. This tool, which looks and works like a pizza cutter, must be used with a self-healing mat and a see-through ruler. Always use the safety shield of the rotary cutter when it is not in use.

Fold the fabric as described on page 16. Keeping this fold in place, lay the fabric on the mat. Place a see-through ruler on the fabric. Align one of the ruler's grid lines with the fold and trim the uneven edge of the fabric. Apply steady, even pressure to the rotary cutter and to the ruler to keep them and the fabric from shifting. Do not let the cutter get farther away from you than the hand that is holding the ruler. Stop cutting and reposition your hand.

Reposition the ruler so that it covers the width of the strip to be cut and the trimmed edge is on the markings for the appropriate measurement on the ruler.

After cutting the strip, hold it up to make sure it is straight. If it is angled, refold the fabric and trim it again. Continue cutting strips, checking frequently that the strips are straight.

t o o l s

A sharp pair of scissors is essential for cutting fabric. Keep another, separate pair of scissors for cutting out templates and other nonfabric uses.

To cut fabric quickly and easily, invest in a rotary cutter, see-through ruler, and self-healing mat. These tools let you cut strips of fabric efficiently.

The needles used for hand piecing and hand appliqué are called sharps. For hand quilting, use betweens (generally, start with a size 8 and work toward using a size 10 or 12). Use the smallest needle you can to make the smallest stitches.

Always use a sharp needle on your sewing machine; a dull needle will tend to skip stitches and snag the threads of your fabric, creating puckers. Use size 9/70 or 11/80 for piecing and appliqué and size 11/80 (in most cases) or 14/90 (for a thick quilt) for machine quilting.

Use fine, sharp straight pins (such as silk pins) for piecing and holding appliqué pieces in place before basting or stitching. Long quilter's pins are used to hold the three layers (top, batting, and backing) before they are basted together or quilted.

h a n d   a p p l i q u é

Prepare pieces of fabric to be appliquéd by hand by tracing around the template on the right side of the fabric. Add a seam allowance as you cut out

each piece. Fold under the seam allowance along the marked seam line. Baste around each piece to hold the seam allowances turned under, clipping curves where necessary.

Pin the first piece to be stitched to the background. Hand stitch it to the background with a blindstitch or, for a more decorative look, use a blanket stitch and contrasting thread. When the appliqué is complete, consider carefully trimming the background fabric from behind the appliqué inside the stitching line. This must be done with great care so that the appliqué is not snipped, but it does reduce the bulk and make it easier to quilt.

machine appliqué

Use fusible webbing to hold the pattern piece firmly in place. Follow the manufacturer's instruc-

tions to bond the webbing to the back of the pattern piece, remove the protective paper, and then bond the pattern piece to the background fabric. Stitch around it using a $^1/_8$-inch- to $^3/_{16}$-inch-wide zigzag stitch. The stitches should be close together, but not so close that the fabric does not feed smoothly through the machine.

quilting

Quilting, stitching that goes through all three layers of the quilt, is both functional and decorative. It holds the batting in place. It is also an important design element, greatly enhancing the texture of the finished quilt. For a traditional

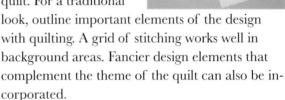

look, outline important elements of the design with quilting. A grid of stitching works well in background areas. Fancier design elements that complement the theme of the quilt can also be incorporated.

Spread out the backing (right side down) on a table or other flat surface. Use masking tape to secure it after smoothing it out. Place the batting on top of the backing, smoothing it out also. Finally, place the completed quilt top on the backing, right side up. Stretch it out and tape it down.

For hand quilting, baste the layers together using long stitches. For best results, start basting at the center of the quilt and work toward the edges. Create a grid of basting by making a line of stitching approximately every four inches.

hand quilting

Hand quilting has a beautiful, classic appearance that cannot be duplicated by machine. To outline-quilt design areas, stitch $^1/_4$-inch away from each seam line. Simply decide where to stitch by eye or use $^1/_4$-inch masking tape placed along each seam

as a guide. Masking tape can also be used as guides for straight lines and grids. Stitch beside the edge of the tape, avoiding stitching through the tape and getting the adhesive on the needle and thread. Do not leave the masking tape on the fabric when you are finished stitching each day, however, because it can leave a sticky residue that is difficult to remove.

Some quilters hold their work unsupported in their lap when they quilt. Most quilters, however, prefer to use some sort of quilting hoop or frame to hold the quilt stretched out. This makes it easier to stitch with an even tension and helps to prevent puckering and tucks.

Use betweens (quilting needles) for hand quilting. The smaller the needle (higher numbers like 11 and 12), the easier it will be to make small stitches. A quilting thimble on the third finger of your quilting hand will protect you from needle sores.

Use no more than 18 inches of quilting thread at once. Longer pieces of thread tend to tangle, and the end gets worn as it is pulled through the fabric. Knot the end of the thread and slip the needle into the quilt top and batting about an inch from where the first stitch should start. Pull the needle up through the quilt top at the beginning of the first stitch. Hold the thread firmly and give it a little tug. The knot should pop into the batting and lodge between the quilt top and backing.

The quilting stitch is a running stitch. Place your free hand (left hand for right-handed people) under the quilt to feel for the needle as it pokes through. Load the needle with a couple of stitches

by rocking the needle back and forth. Keep your stitches small and evenly sized and make sure you are going through all three layers.

binding

Binding may be made from strips of fabric that match or coordinate with the fabrics used in the quilt. These strips may be cut on the straight grain or on the bias. Straight binding is easier to cut and apply. Quilts that have curved edges require bias binding. Also, bias binding is stronger and tends to last longer. You can also purchase quilt binding.

To make straight binding, cut strips of fabric $3^{1}/_{4}$ inches wide on the lengthwise or crosswise grain. For each side of the quilt, you will need a strip the length of that side plus two inches.

Baste around the quilt, $^{1}/_{4}$ inch from the outer edge. Make sure all corners are square and trim any excess batting or fabric. Prepare each strip of binding by folding it in half lengthwise, wrong sides together, and press. Find the center of each strip. Also find the center of each side of the quilt.

Place the binding strip on top of the quilt, aligning the raw edges of the strip and of the quilt and matching the centers. Stitch a $^{1}/_{2}$ inch seam from one end of the quilt to the other. If

you use an even-feed walking foot instead of the regular presser foot, it will be easier to keep the binding and the quilt smooth.

Trim the excess binding from each end. Fold the binding to the back of the quilt and slip stitch it in place. Repeat for the other opposite side of the quilt. Attach the binding to the ends of the quilt using the same procedure except *do not* trim the ends of the binding. Instead, fold the excess binding over the end of the quilt. Holding the end in place, fold the binding to the back of the quilt and slipstitch in place.

making a hanging sleeve

To make a sleeve for hanging a quilt, cut a strip of fabric (muslin or a scrap of backing fabric) 6 inches wide and as long as the quilt is wide. To finish the ends of the strip, roll under the ends to the wrong side of the fabric and slip-stitch (or machine stitch). Fold the fabric lengthwise with wrong sides together. Stitch a $^3/_8$-inch seam the length of the sleeve. Turn the sleeve wrong side out and press the seam. Stitch a $^5/_8$-inch seam over the first seam. Turn the sleeve right side out and press. Stitch the sleeve to the top of the quilt and insert a dowel to hang the quilt.

MAKING A BOW

There are many ways to make bows, and the more you make, the easier it becomes. Follow the instructions, and before long you will be a pro.

1. Crimp the ribbon between thumb and forefinger at the desired streamer length, with the streamer hanging down. Make an equal number of loops on each side of your thumb by crimping each individually while you guide the ribbon into a loop in a circular direction. Crimp each new loop next to the previous one, rather than on top. Secure the loops in the center with wire twisted tightly on the back, leaving the second streamer pointing up.

2. While holding the bow in the same position, roll three inches of that streamer toward you over your thumb, making a small center loop as a knot. If the ribbon has a right and wrong side, twist the loop right side out and catch the loop under your thumb. The streamer will again be pointing up. Bring one end of wire from the back over that streamer beside the knot and to the back again. Twist the wires again. Bring the streamers together beneath the bow and *V* or angle-cut the ends at different lengths.

flowers, flowers everywhere!

How deeply seated in the human is the liking for gardens and gardening.

— *Alexander Smith*

MAGNOLIA ❦ SWAG

Add silk magnolias to a grapevine wreath and greet your guests with the elegance of southern hospitality.

What You'll Need

18- to 24-inch grapevine swag

18-gauge wire

2½ yards gold mesh ribbon, 2 inches wide

Scissors

Fabric glue

Thin wire

Floral picks

Florist tape

Cool-temp glue gun, glue sticks

34-inch silk magnolia stem; 18 to 24 leaves, 1 bud, 2 flowers

3 to 5 vinyl pears, 3 inches each (picks attached)

16 to 24 dried eucalyptus stems, 12 inches each

4 to 8 stems assorted silk green leaves, 12 inches each

8 to 12 silk wheat stems with leaves, 18 inches each

8 to 12 silk baby's breath stems, 18 inches each

1. Cut a length of wire about 8 inches long. To make a hanger, twist wire around a few branches on back of wreath and make a loop.

2. Make a 5-loop bow with tails on either side. Angle-cut ribbon and seal edges with fabric glue. Secure ribbon with a thin wire. Attach to a floral pick; wrap pick with florist tape. Glue bow in center of swag. Attach tails with thin wire (or hot glue) along sides of swag.

3. Remove leaves and blossoms from magnolia stem. Attach flowers to floral picks; wrap with florist tape. Glue blossoms near bow, slightly to the right side of swag. Glue bud to left side of swag. Glue pears around swag in a pleasing manner.

4. Glue eucalyptus leaves around outside edges of swag. Fill in spaces with assorted silk leaves.

5. Glue wheat stems and baby's breath radiating from center of swag.

SPRING · GARDEN · SAMPLER

FLOWERS, FLOWERS EVERYWHERE!

A country cross- stitched sampler will add warmth to any room you hang it in. Personalize this sampler with your favorite gardening phrase!

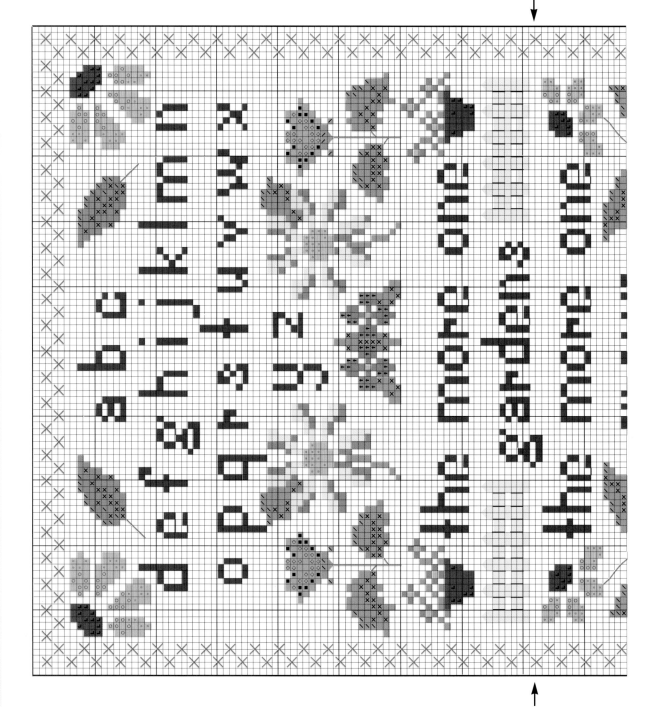

F L O W E R S ,   F L O W E R S   E V E R Y W H E R E !

2 8

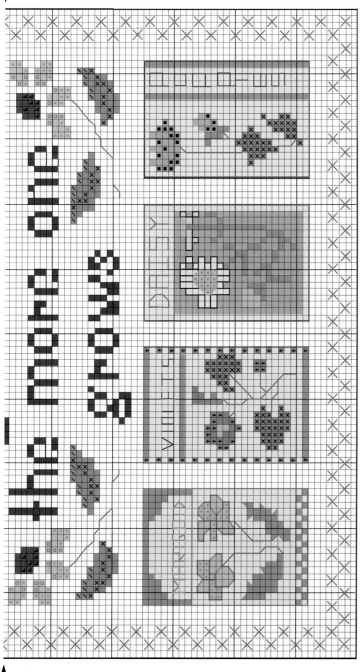

Overlap chart at arrows.

What You'll Need

16×13-inch piece misty taupe cross-stitch cloth, 14 count

#24 tapestry needle

Embroidery floss: see color chart

Stitch according to the directions in the Introduction. Do all cross-stitch and names on seed packets with 2 strands of floss and all other backstitch with 1 strand.

Colors	DMC #
Light green	368
Medium green	320
Dark green	319
Light yellow	727
Medium yellow	725
Gold	783
Light brown	435
Medium brown	433
Light pink	3713
Medium pink	605
Dark pink	961
Light purple	554
Dark purple	552
Light gray	415
White	414
Wildflowers	(variegated)

FLOWERS, FLOWERS EVERYWHERE!

PANSIED ✦ PRESSED ✦ FLOWERS

With these pressed flowers hanging in your kitchen, you can remember that spring is always around the corner!

What You'll Need

3 pansies

Fern leaves

Wax paper

Cardboard

Heavy book

Two 5×7-inch sheets of glass, ⅛-inch thick, (have glass shop drill ⅛-inch holes at top corners of glass)

Glass cleaner

Lint-free cloth

Cotton gloves (optional)

Adhesive copper foil, ½ inch wide

Ruler

Scissors

Copper wire: 14 and 24 gauge

Wire cutters

1. Arrange pansies and ferns on wax paper and cover with a second sheet of paper. Place a piece of cardboard on top. Place layers between pages of a heavy book. Leave book in a warm, dry place for 4 to 6 weeks.

2. Lay the glass on a smooth, dry surface. Clean all sides thoroughly with glass cleaner and lint-free cloth. (Wearing clean cotton gloves will eliminate fingerprints.) Arrange flowers and ferns on a sheet of glass; leave border free so foil strips won't cover flowers. Carefully place second sheet of glass on top.

 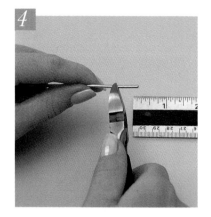 

3. Cut strips of copper foil ½ inch longer than sides of glass. Peel off paper backing and center strip (from front to back of glass) along edge of glass. Press lightly and fold both edges of foil onto glass to adhere. Fold the short ends over and around corners. Repeat on all sides.

4. Cut a 10-inch piece of 24-gauge copper wire. Cut two ½-inch pieces of 14-gauge copper wire for pins.

5. To attach the copper hanging wire, insert the 10-inch length through both holes from the back. Wrap each end of wire tightly around a copper pin to anchor the wire in place.

SUNFLOWER ❦ GARDEN

Extend the warm colors of rustic country fields with this mixture of yellow sunflowers, orange pumpkins, and burgundy Indian corn.

What You'll Need

3¹⁄₂×6¹⁄₂×6¹⁄₂-inch distressed wood crate

3×4×4-inch block dry floral foam

Hot glue gun, glue sticks

Sheet moss

2 to 4 pieces green reindeer moss

Wire cutters

2 stems mustard yellow silk sunflowers, 4- to 5-inch heads each

Mustard yellow silk sunflower spray, with two 2-inch heads and 1 bud

Sunflower seed packet

3-inch silk pumpkin pick

Burgundy mini Indian corn

Metal garden spade

Dried black-eyed Susan head

6 to 8 branches green preserved eucalyptus

4 to 5 wood branches

4 to 5 strands natural raffia

Scissors

1. Glue foam into crate. Cover with moss.

2. Using wire cutters, trim a large sunflower 21 to 22 inches long and insert into middle of crate. Cut second large sunflower 15 to 16 inches long and insert off to right of center. Cut a sunflower off the sunflower spray and trim wire. Cut the spray 10 to 12 inches long and insert into left side of crate.

3. Hot glue the seed packet, trimmed sunflower, pumpkin, and Indian corn into base of crate.

FLOWERS, FLOWERS EVERYWHERE!

4. Hot glue the end of the spade tip and insert into the foam at front left of crate. Hot glue the dried flower head onto spade.

5. Cut eucalyptus 16 to 18 inches long and insert behind sunflowers. Cut shorter pieces of eucalyptus and insert around sides of crate. Insert other branches throughout arrangement. Tie raffia to spade handle.

Tip

You can add a few drops of your favorite fall scented oil inside the moss area of the arrangement to bring in the fragrance of the season.

GARDEN · TOOLS
AND · GLOVES

Your tools can be just as flowery as your garden with a little paint. And these would make a great gift for your favorite gardener!

What You'll Need

Wood or light-colored plastic handle garden tools

Tan garden gloves

Tracing paper

Transfer paper

Pencil

Acrylic paint: holly green, pumpkin, heather, baby pink, blue heaven, lemon yellow

Textile medium

Brushes: #2 flat, 10/0 liner

Stylus

Matte spray finish

1. Trace and apply pattern on handles of tools and top of gloves.

2. For tools, line (with liner brush) and basecoat leaves (with #2 brush) using holly green paint.

3. For gloves only, mix paint with textile medium according to manufacturer's sug-

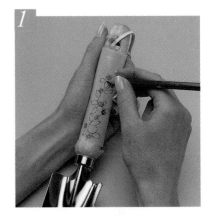

gested directions. Line and basecoat leaves with holly green and textile medium.

4. Using assorted colors (pumpkin, heather, baby pink, blue heaven) and stylus, make 5-dot flowers. Dot center of each flower with lemon yellow.

5. Let dry and spray tool handles (not gloves) with matte spray finish.

Pattern is 100%

LILY ✤ BUD ✤ QUILT

You can grow some beautiful memories with this lily bud crib quilt. Let your talents blossom with this elegant design!

What You'll Need

1³⁄₈ yards white-on-cream fabric

³⁄₈ yard light green calico

¹⁄₄ yard peach/green plaid

³⁄₄ yard peach calico

³⁄₈ yard dark peach

¹⁄₄ yard dark green

1³⁄₄ yards backing fabric

³⁄₈ yard binding fabric

1¹⁄₂ yards light fusible webbing

1 package light fusible strip webbing, ³⁄₈-inch roll

1 package low-loft polyester batting, 45×60 inches

Thread: peach, dark green

1 package sea foam green single-fold bias tape

Quilt ruler

Rotary cutter and self-healing mat

Quilt Dimensions: 39¼×54½

See quilting instructions on page 17–21 of the Introduction.

1. From white-on-cream, cut 21×36-inch rectangle and four 6×45-inch strips. Cut 2 strips to 6×40 inches and 2 strips to 6×35¾ inches. From light green, cut two 11-inch squares; cut on the diagonal, forming 4 triangles.

2. Fuse 7×13-inch piece of webbing to plaid. Remove paper. Cut two 6-inch squares, and cut each on both diagonals, forming 8 triangles (discard 2).

3. From peach calico, cut nine 2¹⁄₂×45-inch strips. Cut 1 strip into two 21-inch pieces and 2 strips into 36-inch pieces. Cut 2 strips into 35¾-inch pieces and 4 strips into 24¾-inch pieces for outer border. Fuse four 2×17-inch pieces of webbing to 4 pieces of peach calico remaining from outer border. Remove paper and cut into four 1¹⁄₂×17-inch strips.

4. Line up strips, 1 on top of the other, 2 right sides up and 2 right sides down. Place on horizontal line of cutting board. Place 45 degree line of ruler on same line and cut. Keeping same angle, move over 2¹⁄₈ inches and cut. Cut 12 parallelograms.

5. From dark peach, cut two 2×45-inch strips and two 2¹⁄₂×45-inch strips. From 1 of the 2¹⁄₂-inch strips, cut ten 2¹⁄₂-inch squares. Cut 2¹⁄₂×15-inch piece from remainder. Cut other 2¹⁄₂-inch strip into three 15-inch pieces. Fuse 2¹⁄₂×15-inch piece of webbing to each of four 15-inch strips. Remove paper and cut each strip to 2¹⁄₈×15 inches. Line up strips, 1 on top of the other, and place on horizontal line of cutting board. Straighten edges. Cut at 2¹⁄₈-inch marking. Cut 20 squares.

6. From two 2×45-inch strips of dark peach, cut four 2×17-inch pieces. Cut four

2×17-inch pieces of webbing and fuse to dark peach pieces. Remove paper and cut each piece to 1½×17 inches. Follow Step 4 and cut 12 parallelograms.

7. From dark green, cut four 2×45-inch strips. From webbing, cut ten 2×17-inch strips. Trim 8 webbing strips to 2×15 inches. Fuse two 2×17-inch pieces of webbing side by side to dark green strip. Using leaf pattern pieces, trace 4 large leaves and 16 small leaves. Cut out and remove paper.

8. Cut each of 3 remaining dark green strips into three 2×15-inch pieces. Fuse 2×15-inch piece of webbing to 8 dark green pieces. Remove paper and cut each of 8 strips to 1½×15 inches. Take 4 strips at a time and follow Step 4, making 1-inch parallelograms. Make 40.

9. From both the bias tape and strip webbing, cut 2

pieces 11¼ inches long and 1 piece 23 inches long. Fuse webbing to tape and remove paper.

10. Fuse strip webbing to long edge of each light green triangle. Remove paper. Place light green triangles on top of white-on-cream center rectangle at corners, match edges, and pin. Triangles will overlap slightly. Fuse triangles and hand baste layers together at edges.

11. Arrange 12 dark peach parallelograms (see photograph). Points are ¼ inch from side edges and just touch green triangles. Fuse. Place peach calico pieces to bottom sides of dark peach and fuse. Outer pieces touch light green triangles.

12. Using ruler, fuse long piece of bias tape between top and bottom flowers. Fuse 2 shorter pieces of bias tape on straight line between side flowers. Center plaid triangles

over bias tape and line them up with rest of flower sections. Fuse. Place 4 large green leaves on a diagonal line and fuse to center.

13. Pin and stitch 2½×36-inch peach calico strip to each side of center section. Press seams toward calico.

14. Stitch dark peach square (unfused) to both ends of 21-inch peach calico strips. Press seams toward squares. Matching seams of corner squares to side seams, pin and stitch to top and bottom.

15. With 6×40-inch strip of white-on-cream, line up 6 buds and 12 leaves on each strip (see photograph). Fuse pieces 1½ inches from each side and each end, leaving 2-inch space in the middle. Repeat. Pin and stitch strips to sides. With 6×35¾-inch strip of white-on-cream, center 4 buds and 8 leaves 1½ inches from top and bottom of each strip. Fuse. Center

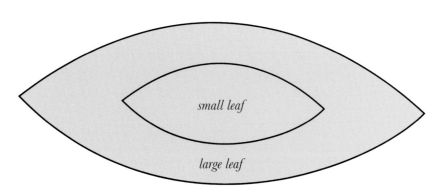

small leaf

large leaf

Patterns are 100%

small green leaves facing diagonally in 5¾-inch area on strip end and fuse. Repeat with remaining 3 leaf sections. Pin and stitch strips to top and bottom.

16. Stitch two 24¾-inch peach calico strips on either side of dark peach square for outer border. Press seams toward squares. Pin and stitch long strips to each side of quilt and press seams toward peach calico.

17. Stitch dark peach square to each end of two 35¾-inch peach calico strips. Press seams toward squares. Matching side seams with square seams, pin and stitch last strips to top and bottom of quilt. Press seams toward peach calico strips.

18. Place backing facedown and center batting. Place quilt top faceup over batting. Pin and hand baste. Starting at center and using dark green thread, straight stitch bias

tape stems on both edges of bias tape. Backstitch at beginning and end of each line of stitching. Change to medium zigzag stitch, and zigzag 4 dark green large leaf edges and long sides of corner triangles.

19. Using peach thread, zigzag stitch around all dark peach and peach calico parallelograms and plaid triangles in center section. Straight stitch around peach calico inner borders and squares. Zigzag dark peach buds around outside. With dark green thread, zigzag around bud leaves and corner diagonal leaf sections.

20. For binding, cut five 2×45-inch strips. Stitch together strips to make 1 long strip. Fold in half lengthwise, wrong sides together. Stitch binding to quilt top, beginning in middle of 1 side and leaving 3 inches of binding free. End stitching ¼ inch from each corner. Begin next side, and repeat for all sides and corners. End stitching about 6 inches before binding ends meet. Stitch ends of binding, trim excess, and finish stitching binding. Trim batting and backing. Miter corners, turn binding to back, and blind stitch in place. Remove basting.

RUSTIC ·🍃· RAKE ·🍃· AND GARDEN ·🍃· SPADE

Splendors of your garden are displayed in this colorful mixture of dried flowers, blooming bulbs, and country clay pots.

What You'll Need

10×27-inch wood rake	Zinnia seed packet
3 terra-cotta pots, two 3-inch and one 2-inch	10 to 12 stems fresh or dried pink statice
Acrylic paint: dark green, gold	Dried purple zinnia head
Small sponge	8 stems yarrow
22-gauge floral wire	10 stems dried poppy pods
Wire cutters	3 to 4 stems dried yellow heather
Metal and wood handle garden spade	5 to 6 stems dried basil lepidium
3×4×8-inch block dry floral foam	3 to 4 stems dried green broom
Hot glue gun, glue sticks	1 or 2 stems fresh or dried lemon leaf (salal)
Sheet moss	3 to 4 branches honey-suckle garland vine
3 garden bulbs	

1. Sponge paint clay pots green. Let dry. Sponge paint pots gold. Let dry.

2. Wire clay pots to center of rake. Wire spade to rake.

3. Cut foam and hot glue pieces inside and around clay pots. Hot glue moss to foam.

4. Hot glue 3 garden bulbs and seed packet onto garden spade. Cut and hot glue statice into clay pots and remaining dried and fresh flowers in and around clay pots and down the handle of the rake.

5. Glue honeysuckle vine throughout the design.

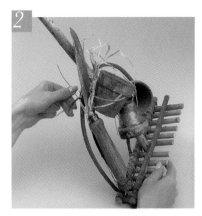

This soft sculptured bunny looks all ready to garden— but she'll hold all your important notes on the refrigerator.

What You'll Need

3-inch muslin bunny

6×2-inch piece of fabric

6-inch length flat lace

Scissors

Sewing machine and thread

Iron

Sewing needle

Miniature gardening tool

Miniature watering can

Tacky glue

Magnet

1. Sew lace to bottom edge of fabric. Iron lace flat if needed. Fold dress in half and sew back seam with ⅛-inch seam allowance. Cut one-inch arm slit at center top of dress (both arm slits will be cut at same time because fabric is folded). Turn dress right side out.

2. Working from back to front, fold arm slit sides in ¼ inch and neckline down ¼ inch. Finger press folds. With needle and thread and using a running stitch, start in the middle of the back and continue through to front neckline. Place dress on bunny; be sure seam is in back. Continue sewing with running stitch to starting place. Gather neckline firmly. Knot off.

3. Tack-stitch gardening tool to one bunny arm. Tack-stitch watering can to other arm.

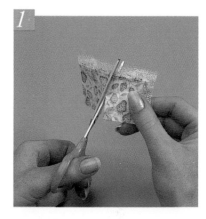

4. Lift dress and dab a small amount of glue on bunny back. Lower dress and press dress into glue. Glue magnet to back of bunny.

FLOWERS, FLOWERS EVERYWHERE!

The
natural
charm of
this
sunflower
bonnet is
filled
with
wonderful
memories
of the
warmth
of
summer.

What You'll Need

17-inch straw hat	4 decorative seed packages
Florist wire	3 dried garlic cloves
Hot glue gun, glue sticks	1 silk pomegranate
Green sheet moss	4 to 6 dried sunflowers
3 to 5 large silk leaves	Red raffia
3 yards sunflower ribbon, 1½ inches wide	3 floral picks
Scissors	1 mushroom bird
Excelsior	Plastic plant stake
3 small plastic or ceramic eggs	Permanent black marker
2½-inch miniature watering can	

1. Stick florist wire through the top of straw hat and twist wire to form a loop. (Top and bottom of hat are references points as if hat were hanging on the wall.) Glue hanger in place.

2. Glue sheet moss around brim of hat. It doesn't need to go on evenly—it should look natural. Glue leaves around hat.

3. Cut ribbon into 1-yard and 2-yard pieces and *V*-cut all ends. From the 2-yard piece, make a 6-loop florist bow with 12-inch tails (see page 21). In center of bow, glue a small nest of excelsior. Glue eggs to middle of excelsior. Glue bow to bottom of hat.

F L O W E R S ,   F L O W E R S   E V E R Y W H E R E !

4. Wrap florist wire around handle of watering can and push stems of wire through hat. Twist wire on underside of hat to secure. You may want to hot glue watering can to hat for extra security.

5. Glue seed packages around hat. Glue garlic cloves at top and right side of hat and pomegranate next to cloves on top of hat.

6. Glue sunflowers around hat. Cut 4-inch lengths of red raffia and attach 15 to 20 strands to each of 3 floral picks. Glue a pick underneath bow, a pick above watering can, and a pick to right of garlic cloves.

7. Cut remaining ribbon into 2 unequal pieces. Glue streamers up crown of hat and spot glue in place. Glue a small nest of sheet moss above longest streamer and glue bird to top of nest.

8. Write "SUNFLOWER" on plant stake and glue stake to left side of brim, above watering can.

SILK · RIBBON · HEART

Create this enchanting floral heart to hang in a room where you want that extra-special romantic touch.

What You'll Need

8$^1/_2$×7$^1/_2$-inch piece monoco fabric, 28 count

4mm silk embroidery ribbon (see color chart)

Large-eyed embroidery needle

Plain white paper

#2 pencil

Embroidery hoop (optional)

Scissors

Needle

Thread

Colors	Offray #
French blue	332
Buttermilk	824
Sweet nectar	161
Moss	570
Rosewood	169
Iris	447
Moonstone	203

When using an embroidery hoop, protect your fabric by placing two pieces of thin white cloth between the fabric and hoop. Cut a hole in the middle of each piece of cloth large enough to expose the pattern area. Place a piece on each side of the fabric you will be embroidering, with the holes over your work area, and place all layers in embroidery hoop. Always take work out of the hoop when you are not working on the project.

Transfer pattern to plain white paper and tape to a sunny window. Trace pattern onto fabric using the #2 pencil. Use 12-inch pieces of ribbon when embroidering. Embroider design in the following order: roses with sweet nectar; blue flowers using French blue and straight stitch; daisies using rosewood and French knots; wisteria using iris and French knots; stems using moss and stem stitch; leaves using moss and straight stitch. (See finished photograph for color placement.) With needle and thread, sew loose ends of ribbon to other ribbon so that ends do not show.

For stitch illustrations and information, see pages 11–14 of the Introduction.

Pattern is 100%

FLOWERS, FLOWERS EVERYWHERE!

If fences make good neighbors, then this wreath will make a great gift for your favorite next-door friend!

What You'll Need

14-inch grapevine wreath

18-gauge wire

6-inch wooden gate

White acrylic paint

Paintbrush

3½-inch clay pot

46 inches floral print ribbon, 2½ inches wide

Scissors

Fabric glue

Floral picks

Florist tape

3 strands natural raffia, 36 inches each

3½×3½-inch block floral foam

Cool-temp glue gun, glue sticks

Wood straw

3-inch mushroom bird

2½-inch nest

3 stems green vinyl ivy, 18 inches each

12 stems assorted silk florals with leaves: white, pink, blue

4-inch birch wreath

1-inch egg

1. Cut a length of wire about 8 inches long. To make a hanger, twist wire around a few branches on back of wreath and make a loop.

2. Paint gate white. Let dry. Paint rim of clay pot white. Let dry.

3. Angle-cut ribbon into 10-inch and 36-inch pieces. Seal ribbon ends with fabric glue. Make a 2-loop bow from 36-inch piece of ribbon. Secure with wire. Attach ribbon to a floral pick; wrap pick with florist tape. Place a wire in the center of the remaining piece of ribbon and attach to a floral pick; wrap pick with florist tape. Set ribbons aside. From raffia, make a 3-loop bow with long tails. Secure bow with wire and attach to a floral pick; wrap pick with florist tape. Set aside.

6. Glue stems of flowers around ivy. Place larger flowers near bottom of wreath.

7. Glue ribbon under fence. Wire tails along each side of wreath. Glue remaining tails near bottom of wreath.

8. Gently separate 4-inch birch wreath. Attach birch pieces to picks; wrap picks with florist tape. Glue birch pieces into wreath and pot.

9. Glue raffia bow and egg into left side of pot.

4. Wire fence to left side of wreath. Glue floral foam into pot. Cover top of foam with wood straw. Glue a floral pick into bottom of bird; insert bird into nest. Glue nest into top right side of pot. Wire clay pot to right front of fence.

5. Glue a stem of ivy up left side of wreath. Cut remaining ivy into smaller pieces and glue around lower right side, bottom, and left side of wreath.

MIRRORED · FLOWERS
FRAME

Mirror, mirror on the wall— this mirror is the fairest of all! Add silk pansies to a plain frame for a beautiful addition to your foyer.

What You'll Need

Picture frame

Green sheet moss

Hot glue gun, glue sticks

2 yards pansy ribbon

9 silk pansies

Assorted small dried flower heads: larkspur, globe amaranth, American statice, ammobium

Assorted dried fillers: sweet Annie, plumosa, myrtle leaves

1. Glue moss over front of frame; some moss can hang over sides.

2. Make 4 small bows and hot glue a bow in each corner.

3. Glue a silk pansy to center of each bow. Add a pansy at the top and bottom of frame between bows.

4. On one side of frame, glue on a pansy. On other side, glue on 2 pansies.

5. Hot glue remaining assorted flowers and fillers on frame. For an extra touch, sprinkle with your favorite essential oil scent.

VICTORIAN · BASKET

A soft delicate collar of lace surrounds this basket. The profusion of colors, shapes, and sizes of flowers creates a Victorian touch of beauty.

What You'll Need

Round basket

3½ feet lace ribbon (3× circumference of basket)

Hot glue gun, glue sticks

Dry floral foam

Knife

Green sheet moss

Craft pins

22-gauge stem wire

Wire cutters

3 blue hydrangeas

3 pink roses

7 pansies

3 purple dried-look asters with buds

3 pink dried-look asters with buds

4 stems cream statice

2 cream sweet William with buds

2 cream/burgundy sweet William with buds

1. Using glue gun, glue ribbon around lip of basket, gathering ribbon as you go. Cut floral foam to fit basket. Using craft pins, cover foam with sheet moss. Cut 2 pieces of wire twice the height of the floral foam plus 10 inches. Bend wire into a large *U* shape and push this up through basket and into foam about a third of the way from the end. With both ends of wire protruding from foam, twist wire ends together and conceal ends in moss. Repeat with other wire on other end of foam.

2. Glue all flowers before placing into foam. To establish perimeter of design, place blue hydrangeas and pink roses around sides. Use wire cutters to cut flowers to desired lengths.

3. Place pansies and asters to create a rounded shape. Place a few flowers around the perimeter also. If stems of flowers are too short, add length by taping floral picks to stems.

4. Fill in design with statice and sweet William.

cornucopia
of delights

This rule in gardens ne'er forget

To sow dry and set wet.

— *John Ray*

VEGETABLE ❦ FRUIT ❦ BASKET

CORNUCOPIA OF DELIGHTS

6 2

What You'll Need

12×6½-inch oval bark basket

Dry floral foam, 12×6½-inch piece

Craft knife

Cool-temp glue gun, glue sticks

Green garden moss

2 green vinyl ivy stems, 18 inches each

Floral picks

Florist tape: brown, green

Floral wire

Pencil

2 assorted color grape stems, 12 inches each

3 red vinyl apples, 2½ inches each

6 to 12 stems assorted vinyl fruits and vegetables with leaves (figs, squash, cut plums, etc.)

3-inch dried artichoke

2 to 4 stems dried red, orange, or yellow peppers, 1 to 3 inches each

6 to 12 stems dried yellow yarrow

2 to 4 stems dried blue or purple hydrangeas

4-inch birch wreath

12-inch straight birch bunch (2 to 4 stems secured with tape)

1. Cut floral foam to fit basket. Glue into place and cover foam with moss.

2. Separate ivy stems into 8 to 12 pieces. Attach each piece to a pick; secure with florist tape. Insert ivy around edge of basket.

3. To make wrapped wire squiggles, wrap thin wires tightly with brown or green florist tape. Wind wrapped wire around a ¼- to ⅓-inch wooden dowel or pencil.

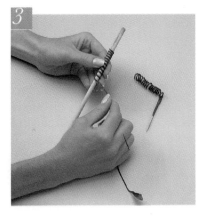

4. Remove wrapped wire and attach to a wooden pick. Secure with florist tape. Insert into arrangement.

5. Separate fruit into individual pieces. Keep grapes in small bunches. Attach each piece to a pick and secure with florist tape. Insert fruit into basket in a pleasing manner. Let some fruit hang over the sides.

6. Insert fig and artichoke. Divide peppers into smaller bunches. Attach each bunch to a pick and secure with florist tape; insert peppers into arrangement. Let some peppers hang over sides.

7. Separate yarrow and hydrangeas into small bunches. Attach each to a pick and secure with florist tape. Fill in remaining spaces in arrangement.

8. Gently separate birch wreath. Attach birch pieces to picks and secure with florist tape. Insert birch into arrangement; let some loop over sides. Insert straight birch sticks near center.

GARDEN SHIRT

Add
quilted
patchwork
squares
to give
old-fashioned
appeal
to this
simple
chambray
shirt.

What You'll Need

Chambray shirt

Tracing paper

Pencil

Cardboard

Craft knife

Washable fabric pen

¼ yard blue and white fabric

⅜ yard garden print fabric

Scissors

Sewing machine

Coordinating thread

Iron

2 pieces cotton batting, 5¾×11¾ inches each

⅜ yard fusible webbing

Quilting thread, needle

1. Trace template pattern (on page 68) onto cardboard and cut out. Cut out center rectangle with craft knife. When using template, outside edge is cutting line and inside edge is stitching line.

2. Using template and fabric pen, trace and cut 6 blue and white rectangles. Trace and cut 6 garden print rectangles, using template to frame garden motifs.

3. Lay out rectangles on shirt to create a checkerboard effect; use 6 rectangles for each side of shirt.

4. Working on one side, divide rectangles into 3 rows (top, middle, bottom). Sew each pair together on stitching line (¼-inch seam allowance). Press seams open.

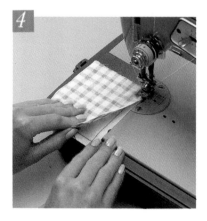

5. Lay pairs out to form checkerboard. Sew top pair to center pair matching seam lines, then sew bottom pair to center pair matching seam lines. Press seams open.

6. Press edges under ¼ inch on all sides. Fit cotton batting rectangles inside pressed edges. Press edges again.

7. Cut fusible webbing to cover entire back of rectangle, including pressed edges. Fuse webbing in place. Remove paper.

8. Place rectangles on front of shirt and fuse. You may need to fuse from the front and back of shirt because of added thickness.

9. Topstitch close to edges on all sides. Stitch on top of all seams (called stitch in ditch).

10. Using needle and quilting thread, outline garden objects with small running quilt stitches (sew through all layers).

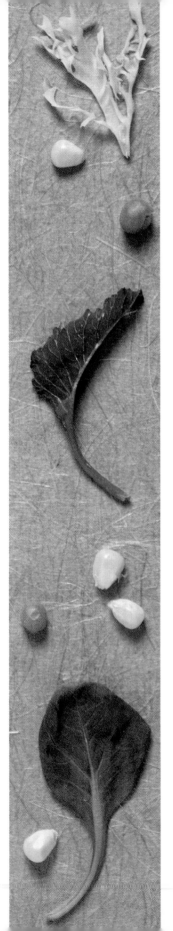

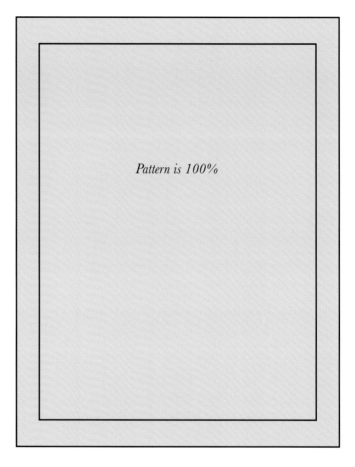

Pattern is 100%

COPPER ✦ PLANT ✦ MARKERS

What You'll Need

3 pieces tooling copper, $3^5/_8 \times 5^7/_{16}$ each

3 pieces wood, $3^5/_8 \times 5^7/_{16}$ each

Wood sealer

Brushes: $^3/_4$ inch flat, #1 liner, #4 round

3 paint stirring sticks

Acrylic paint: midnite green

Gloss paint: Christmas green, metallics silver, gloss black, gloss white, cadmium yellow, Christmas red, orange

Tracing paper

Pencil (with good eraser)

Ruler

Scissors

0000 steel wool

Newspapers

Stylus

Cotton balls

Clear silicone glue

12 bronze thumbtacks

Hammer

Paper towels

1. Seal wood with wood sealer, using largest brush. Let dry. Basecoat paint sticks with midnite green. When dry, paint 1 or 2 coats of Christmas green.

2. Copy designs (on pages 72 and 73) onto tracing paper; add ½-inch borders. Extend outside design lines to edges, making a square in each corner.

3. Gently rub fronts and backs of copper with steel wool. Fold newspaper several thicknesses. Place design on top of copper and place on newspaper. Imprint design with stylus, including border lines. Remove pattern.

4. Turn copper over. To make imprint more pronounced, trace on both sides of all lines and dots of design with stylus. Add scribble lines along border with stylus. Shape roots and radish and onion tops by pressing with a

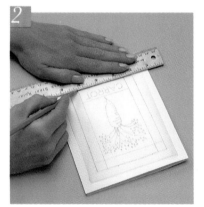

pencil eraser. Turn to front. With stylus, press dots in background around vegetables.

5. Glue balls of cotton to backs of root sections to keep them rounded. Apply glue to one side of board and place copper on top. With small hammer, pound a thumbtack in each corner in front. If copper has stretched, bend excess copper over edge.

6. Use liner brush for smaller areas and #4 brush for other areas. Paint metallics silver along borders and around letters, keeping paint very wet. When borders

are tacky, pat with paper towel to remove some silver. Paint dotted background gloss black.

7. Paint vegetable tops Christmas green. When still wet, add gloss white and touches of cadmium yellow and blend along carrot and radish stems, on midsection of onion, and on a few onion tops. Paint onion root gloss white. Blend Christmas red and cadmium yellow along edges. Paint radish root Christmas red and highlight with gloss white. Paint carrot root orange and blend Christmas red along left side and gloss white on root tip.

Highlight with gloss white. Paint border stripes and lettering Christmas green. Let dry.

8. Glue sticks to back with top edges even.

Patterns are 100%

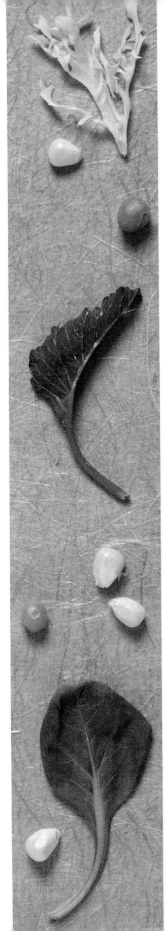

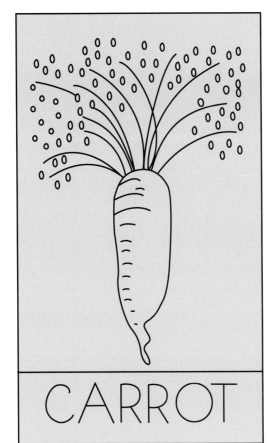

CARROT

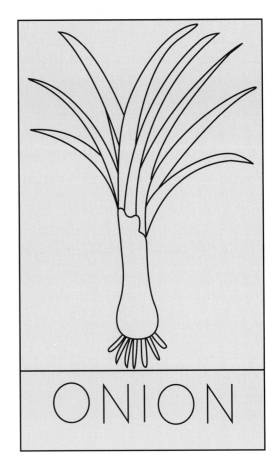

ONION

RADISH

Indulge yourself with fresh carrots any time of the year! These fun carrots make a great table centerpiece.

What You'll Need

½ yard orange fabric (for 20 carrots)

Scrap paper and pencil

Scissors

Pins

Sewing machine

Orange thread

Fiberfill

Stuffing stick (chopstick, unsharpened pencil, etc.)

12×3-inch piece heavy cardboard

Skeins of light, medium, and dark green textured yarn

Sewing needle

1. Trace several carrot patterns (on page 77) onto scrap paper. Cut out patterns from paper. Fold orange fabric twice. Pin paper carrot patterns and cut carrots out of fabric.

2. Fold fabric carrot in half lengthwise. Sew side seam with sewing machine threaded with orange thread. Repeat this step for remaining carrots. Vary seam allowance using ⅛, ¼, and ⅜ inches. Use large, medium, and small carrot patterns with different seam allowances for different size carrots.

3. Trim excess fabric from side seam. Clip tip of fabric carrot. Turn carrot right side out. Stuff carrot with fiberfill—use small amounts of fiberfill at a time. Use chopstick or unsharpened pencil to push fiberfill into carrot. Stuff carrot firmly until almost full.

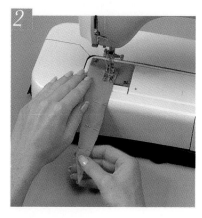

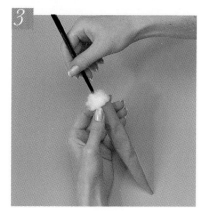

4. Wrap yarns (all three colors at the same time) around yarn template (cardboard). Cut yarn off template from one end. Gather 12 to 20 strands. Holding all strands, tie a knot in center of strands, pulling yarn tightly. For variety in carrot tops, vary the number of strands used for each carrot top. Repeat this step for each carrot.

5. Fold unfinished edge of top of carrot down ½ inch. Starting at seam, sew a running stitch around top of fabric carrot. Insert a carrot top into stuffed carrot cavity. Pull running stitch tight. Knot off. Repeat this step for remaining carrots. Trim carrot top yarn if desired.

6. Assemble carrots in a decorative basket with gardening tools, gloves, seed packets, and other gardening equipment for a decorative centerpiece.

Patterns are 100%

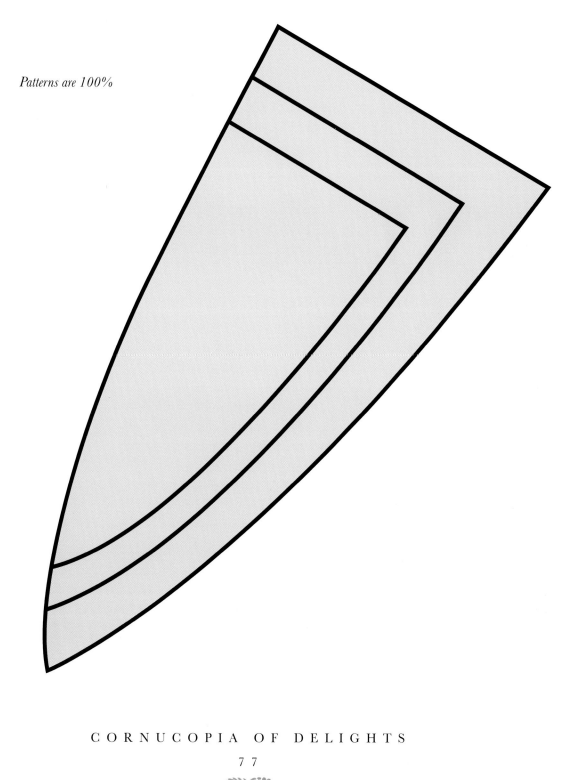

T U R N I P · G A R D E N · G L O V E S

The turnip has a pleasing form with elegant colors; what a suitable decorative theme for gardener's gauntlets!

What You'll Need

1 pair gardener's soft leather gloves

Tracing paper

Pencil

Scissors

Stiff cardboard

#1 knitting needle

Very fine sandpaper

1 or 2 small medium-soft watercolor brushes

Leather acrylic paint: white, fuchsia, blue, green

Dimensional paint: antique gold

1. Trace and cut out turnip pattern.

2. Cut 2 pieces of stiff cardboard to fit inside glove cuff. Insert cardboard and stretch glove flat. Use knitting needle and pattern to make 3 turnip impressions on cuff of each glove.

3. Lightly sand leather inside outlines. You should not see a significant change in appearance of leather.

4. Paint turnips in the following layers: Fill in outline with a solid white coat of paint. Let dry 1 hour. Add second coat if necessary.

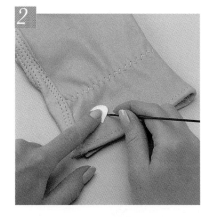

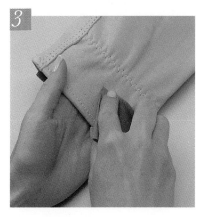

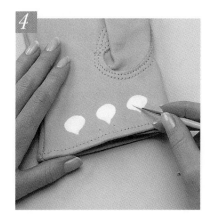

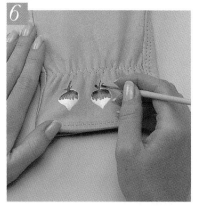

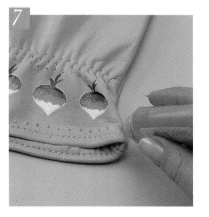

5. Paint top half of turnip fuchsia. Leaving a small white line at the top will add contrast if your glove is dark leather. Let dry at least 1 hour. Using white and fuchsia paint, mix a light pink color. Apply hatching strokes where white and fuchsia meet. Mix blue and fuchsia paints. Apply to the top ⅓ of the turnip. Let dry.

6. Paint a blue stroke across the top of each turnip. Let dry. Add leaves. Let dry.

7. Use the stitching on the glove cuff as a guide to add 2 rows of evenly spaced gold dots with the dimensional paint. Let dry overnight.

COUNTRY ❧ APPLE ❧ BASKET

CORNUCOPIA OF DELIGHTS

81

A-tisket,

a-tasket,

a country

apple

basket!

And it's

just the

right size

for carrying

everything

from

apples to

craft

supplies.

What You'll Need

Woven basket

Brushes: 1-inch flat, #4 round, #10 flat, #0 liner

Dark walnut stain

Paper towels

Acrylic paint: red oxide, unbleached titanium, apricot, burnt umber, hooker's green

Brown paper bag

Tracing paper

Transfer paper

Pencil

Spray varnish

See pages 7–9 of the Introduction for decorative painting instructions.

1. Basket should be smooth and free of dust. Stain basket and lid using 1-inch flat brush and dark walnut stain. Wipe off excess stain with paper towel. Paint top of handles with red oxide. Sand lid with piece of brown paper bag when dry.

2. Transfer pattern to lid top. Use #4 round brush to fill in large apple and edges of other two with red oxide. Fill in lightest areas with unbleached titanium and remaining areas with apricot. Paint seeds burnt umber.

3. Double load #10 flat brush (or #4 round brush) with red oxide and apricot. With apricot side out, paint a highlight on edges of apples. Fill in solid highlight with apricot (upper right side of large apple).

4. Double load brush with burnt umber and apricot to fill in stems. Use apricot to fill in top circle of stem.

5. Fill in flower petals with unbleached titanium. Fill in flower center with apricot. Double load brush with apricot and red oxide to shade the center. Use #0 liner to paint thin lines around and inside the petals.

6. Double load brush with hooker's green and unbleached titanium to fill in the leaves and stems.

7. Use end of brush dipped in unbleached titanium to make dots in clusters of three. You may also add dots on basket, staggering groups of dots in middle two rows of weaving (see finished photo). Allow to dry and spray with 2 to 3 coats of varnish.

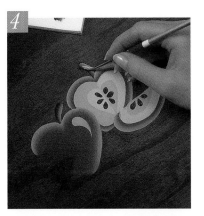

Tips

Let your imagination go—there are many different ways this basket design can be painted. For a natural look, seal the wood with a clear wood sealer instead of a dark color. Perhaps you may want to use pastel colors. Cut the design into different sections and piece together to fit other wood pieces you'd like to paint.

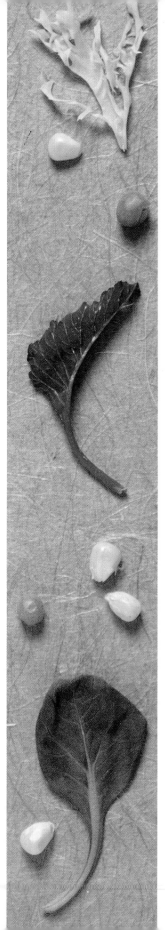

GARDEN · TOOLS · PIN
AND · EARRING · SET

Any green-thumbed gardener would love to have this set of green garden tool jewelry!

What You'll Need

5 miniature green garden tools

5 short eyepins

Wire-cutting pliers

Pushpin

Glue suitable for metal and wood

5 small jump rings

1 kilt pin with 3 loops

1 pair ear clips or wires

1. Using wire cutters, trim shafts of eyepins so shanks measure between $\frac{1}{8}$ to $\frac{3}{16}$ inches long.

2. Use pushpin to make a hole in top of each miniature handle. The hole should be centered and large enough to allow eyepin to fit in up to the eye.

3. Dip an eyepin's shaft in glue; put it in hole of a tool. Let dry thoroughly. Repeat for each tool.

4. Open a jump ring. Insert it in an eyepin and then hang onto loop of kilt pin. Close ring. Repeat with 2 other tools for kilt pin.

5. Open a jump ring, hang a tool and an earring on it. Close ring. Repeat for other earring.

VEGGIE ❦ FLOOR ❦ MAT

This mat will entice people out to your garden; it would also look great as a wall hanging in your family room or sunporch!

What You'll Need

Canvas floor mat, 24×35 inches

Yardstick

Medium and hard pencils

Triangle

Eraser

1-inch masking tape

Small, flat sponge

Acrylic paints: buttermilk, hauser light green, pumpkin, leaf green, olive green, cadmium orange, cadmium yellow

Transfer paper

Tracing paper

Brushes: 2-inch flat, #4 shader, #8 shader, #1 liner, #3 round

Permanent gold marker

Polyurethane varnish

Paint thinner

See pages 7–9 of the Introduction for decorative painting techniques.

1. Using 2-inch brush, paint canvas buttermilk. Let dry overnight.

2. For borders, use medium pencil and measure from top and bottom edges and draw lines at: 1 inch, 1½ inches, 2 inches, 3¼ inches, 3¾ inches, and 4¼ inches. Lightly draw lines. To find placement of center rectangle, lay yardstick diagonally across mat from edge of last top ruled line on right side to last bottom ruled line on left side. Draw a 2-inch line at center. Repeat in opposite direction and draw another line, forming an X. Center of X is center of the corn rectangle. Measure 3¼ inches from right and left sides of center and 4 inches from top and bottom of center. Draw a rectangle, using triangle. Measure 1 inch around all sides of center rectangle and draw a border. Position remaining 6½×8 inch rectangles 3 inches from border and 2¾ inches from sides. Draw 1-inch borders around all rectangles. Erase unnecessary lines.

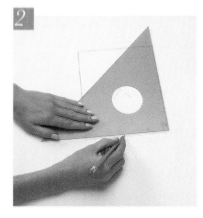

3. Tape around inside and outside edges of rectangles and around ½-inch border strips (at top and bottom of mat). Burnish tape with fingernail. Sponge hauser light green stripes and pumpkin rectangles. Let dry. Remove tape. Outline all lines with gold marker.

4. Trace patterns (on pages 91–93) onto tracing paper, including lines on lettering. Tape words in place, aligning lines on paper with those on canvas. With hard pencil, transfer words only. Transfer vegetables to rectangles, centering designs.

5. Fill in lettering with leaf green, using #1 and #4 brushes. Let dry. Erase pencil lines.

6. With #3 round brush, basecoat carrot tops, corn husks, areas around peas, pea stems, and outside of pods with leaf green. Basecoat pod

edge lines olive green, carrots cadmium orange, and corn cadmium yellow. Dry brush corn silk olive green. Leave tiny lines of buttermilk between objects of the same color that join (such as husk of corn).

7. Using hauser light green, dry brush over pea pods, leaving bottoms darker. Shade vines and top of middle pod, add additional dots and lines to carrot tops, and make thin vertical lines on corn husks.

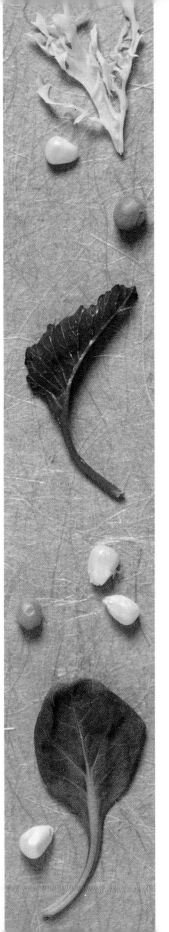

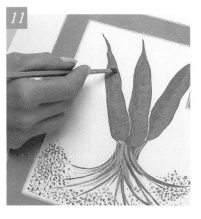

8. Use olive green to continue shading pea pods closer to tops, vines, and carrot stems.

9. Create shading on bottom of peas with leaf green, and highlights on top of peas with olive green; blend colors in centers of peas. Soften pod center lines with a wash of leaf green.

10. Mix leaf green and pumpkin to make khaki brown and outline corn kernels. Wash khaki over kernels on both sides, leaving center of cob clear. Highlight center kernel tops with buttermilk, blend mix of buttermilk and cadmium yellow into kernel centers, and wash khaki onto bottoms. Dot a few areas between kernels with hauser light green and pumpkin. Use khaki and buttermilk to shape top of corn and enhance corn silk lines. Wash over husk with hauser light green, making sure lines remain. Wash bottom section with leaf green.

11. With #4 brush, dry brush pumpkin over carrots, starting at left edge and working to right, leaving some cadmium orange showing. Highlight center of carrots with mix of pumpkin and buttermilk. Define ridges and make a few hairs at root ends with cadmium orange with #1 brush. Let dry overnight.

12. Varnish as directed on can.

CARROTS

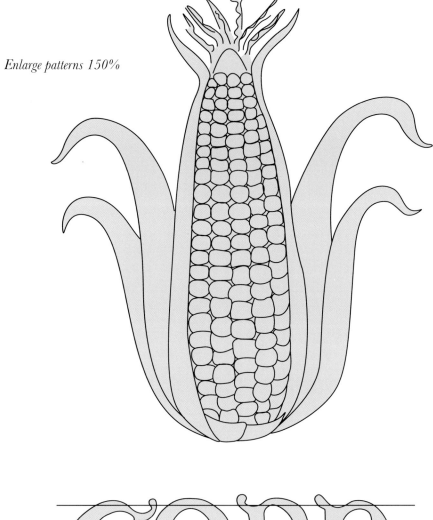

Enlarge patterns 150%

CORN

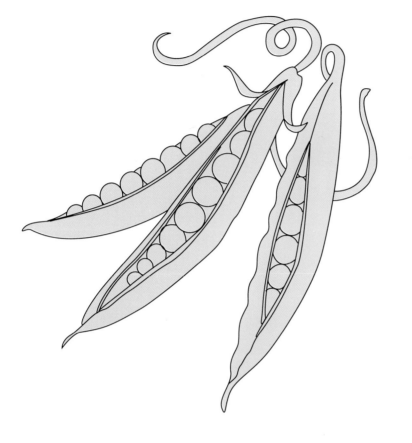

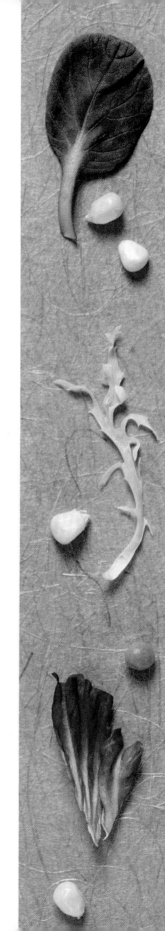

SEED ❧ PACKETS ❧ APRON

Protect your clothes while tending to your garden with this stylish apron. A must for the gardener who has everything!

What You'll Need

Canvas apron

Seed packets wall stencils

Acrylic paint: ultramarine, calico red, evergreen, school bus yellow

Textile medium

³/₈-inch stencil brushes

See stenciling instructions on page 9 of the Introduction.

1. Prewash apron before painting. Do not use fabric softener. Mix all paints with textile medium as directed on bottle.

2. Center stencil A on bottom of apron. Place stencil on apron to determine the number of seed packets that will be stenciled. Prepare ultramarine paint and textile medium. Using a ³/₈-inch stencil brush, wipe off excess paint and dab paint on designated area. Overlap stencil as necessary, continuing pattern across bottom of apron. Let dry. Using only checker border, mask off remaining stencil. Stencil blue border across top of apron. Let dry.

3. Line up stencil B and prepare school bus yellow with textile medium. Apply paint to designated areas. Let dry.

4. Line up stencil C and prepare evergreen and textile medium. Apply paint to designated areas. Let dry.

5. Line up stencil D and prepare calico red with textile medium. Apply paint to designated areas. Let dry. Follow textile medium's manufacturer's instructions for heat setting, if necessary.

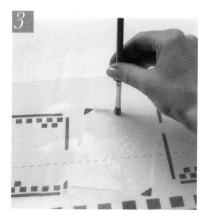

garden party

The love of gardening is a seed that once sown never dies.

— Gertrude Jekyll

IVIED · PATIO · SET

GARDEN PARTY

9 8

Make your outdoor setting as beautiful as it is comfortable! Stencil placemats, director's chairs, and a bug candle for a fresh approach to garden furniture.

What You'll Need

Air painting kit (includes air painter, ivy stencil, true blue tint, eggshell and holiday green paint)

Stencil adhesive (optional)

Masking tape

Paper towels

Canvas director's chair

Cloth placemats

Citronella bucket candle

1. Prewash fabric that will be laundered; don't use fabric softeners. For the director's chair and placemats: Spray back of stencil with adhesive, following manufacturer's instructions. Position and press stencil on surface. Use paper towels and masking tape to cover other exposed surfaces. Assemble air painter onto paint bottle, following manufacturer's directions. Always practice spraying on paper towels first. Using true blue tint, lightly dust center of each ivy leaf.

2. Change to holiday green and spray entire stencil area.

Do not spray heavily. The blue will show slightly to give more shade and dimension to leaves. Remove stencil.

3. For the candle: Base bucket with eggshell. Because the paint will run easily on this surface, spray lightly and let dry. Spray another coat if needed. When stenciling, place the center of the stencil low and wrap stencil around bucket. Cover all other areas with paper towel and masking tape. Hold bucket upright and spray ivy as previously instructed.

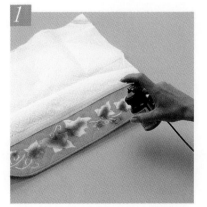

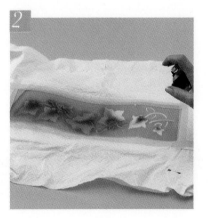

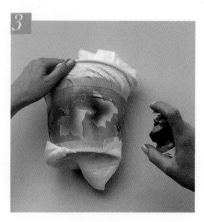

SUMMER · GARDEN · BASKET

GARDEN PARTY

100

This charming Victorian basket has a subtle combination of fragrant fresh and dried blooms of heather, statice, roses, caspia, and hydrangea.

What You'll Need

6×4×9-inch cream basket

11 to 12 stems dried yellow roses

11 stems fresh or dried purple statice

11 stems fresh or dried caspia

11 stems fresh or dried pink heather

3 to 4 stems fresh or dried lemon leaf (salal)

12 to 14 stems dried pink larkspur

12 stems dried green lepidium

12 stems dried green broom

1 package dried white campo flowers

7 to 10 stems dried hydrangea

22-gauge floral wire

Wire cutters

Hot glue gun, glue sticks

Sheet moss

1. Cut all dried and fresh flowers from 7 to 10 inches long. Wire mixture of flowers into 11 to 12 bundles.

2. Slip wire ends of flower bundles through open slats of basket rim and twist wire ends securely inside basket. Overlap each flower bundle onto basket rim as you wire. Secure bundles with hot glue if necessary.

3. Clip excess wire ends and hot glue moss over any exposed wire inside basket.

Tip

Color intensity, quality, and selection is more readily available when using fresh flowers and foliage appropriate for drying. By allowing the fresh flowers to dry naturally in a week or less, your results will be a beautiful permanent display.

SALSA ❦ FIESTA ❦ SHIRT

Add some spice to your life— and to your wardrobe! This saucy shirt is easy to make and oh so fun to wear. Olé!

What You'll Need
❧

White cotton shirt (if shirt has front pocket, remove carefully using seam ripper)

White paper

Pencil

Scissors

Fabric scraps in green, yellow, and red

Lightweight iron-on adhesive

Iron

Ironing board

Straight pins

Sewing machine

Medium rickrack in red and orange

Thread to match fabrics and rickrack

Yellow buttons matching the size and number of button holes on the shirt

1. Trace and cut out patterns (see page 105). Cut fabric into rectangular shapes about ½ inch larger all around than pattern. Cut iron-on adhesive to match each piece of fabric. Following manufacturer's instructions, fuse adhesive to wrong side of fabric. (Be sure iron-on adhesive is appropriate for machine appliqué projects.)

2. Draw around patterns on paper backing. Be sure to reverse pattern from the way you want it to look on shirt. Cut out.

3. Remove paper backing. Lay appliqués on shirt. Pin in place and try shirt on to determine if placement is appropriate. Adjust if necessary.

4. Fuse appliqués to shirt according to manufacturer's instructions.

5. Set sewing machine for an appliqué stitch (a close, narrow zigzag). Place sheet of white paper under shirt and stitch around all appliqués using matching thread colors. (The paper will help keep fabric from puckering as you stitch.) For tomato, stitch red portion first, then green.

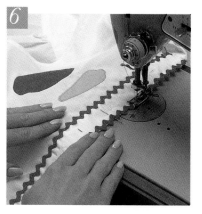

6. Turn under edge of orange rickrack. Match folded edge with top of button placket, to left of buttonholes. Using a straight machine stitch, sew rickrack in place down front of shirt. As you near bottom, trim rickrack about ½ inch beyond edge of shirt. Fold cut end under and continue sewing rickrack, backstitching to hold end secure. Repeat for opposite side of button placket.

7. Turn under edge of red rickrack. Match folded edge with top front edge of collar.

Fold under small part of rickrack at point of collar and use pin to secure until it has been sewn. Use a straight machine stitch to sew rickrack in place around edge of collar. End on opposite side of collar by cutting rickrack about ½ inch longer than necessary and folding edge under to match top of collar. Continue sewing, backstitching end to hold it securely.

8. Remove white buttons from shirt and replace with yellow buttons sewn on with green thread.

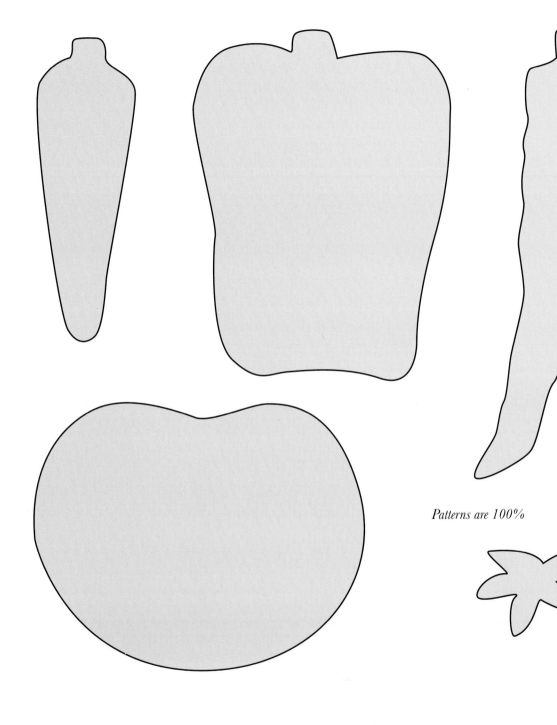

Patterns are 100%

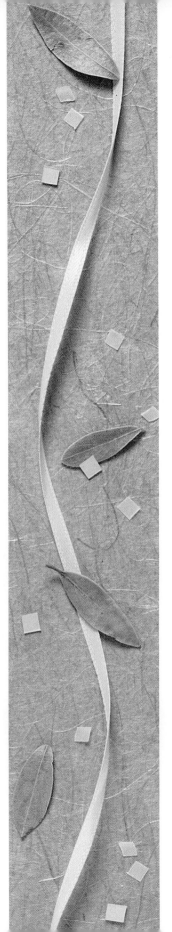

LEMONADE · PITCHER
AND · GLASSES

Make that summer thirst-quenching treat even more special. Lemonade never tasted so good!

What You'll Need

Clear glass pitcher and tall glasses

Pencil

White paper

Scissors

Sticky notes

Overhead projector pen

Cotton swabs

Acrylic enamel paints: cadmium yellow, lemon yellow, true blue

Brushes: liner, ¼-inch flat

Palette

1. Wash and dry glasses and pitcher. Painting must be done on a clean, oil-free surface.

2. Trace lemon patterns (see page 108) onto white paper. Cut out. Trace patterns onto sticky notes at sticky edge and cut out. For pitcher, lay lemon patterns on sticky edge of sticky notes and draw a line around them about ⅛ inch larger than patterns on all sides.

3. Stick lemon, lemon slice, and lemon wedge patterns onto glass surface about 2 inches from bottom (3 inches for pitcher). Draw around patterns with overhead projector pen. Move patterns and repeat. Continue until entire glass has been circled. If there are any stray pen marks on glass inside traced patterns, carefully remove with slightly damp cotton swab.

4. Squirt small amount of cadmium yellow paint onto palette. Using flat brush, fill in lemons with paint. Be careful not to touch traced outline with paintbrush. Use liner brush to paint along curved edge of lemon wedges. For lemon slices, paint circle then put dot in center and paint five spokes radiating out to form lemon segments. Let dry 1 hour before applying second coat of paint.

5. Squirt a small puddle of lemon yellow paint onto palette. Fill in remaining portions of lemon wedges and slices. Let dry 1 hour and apply second coat. If more coats of paint are necessary, be sure to let paint dry 1 hour between coats.

6. Carefully remove pen lines with slightly damp cotton swab.

7. Pour small amount of blue paint onto clean palette.

Use flat brush to paint a checkerboard pattern about ½ inch from bottom of glass. (Use thick layer of glass at bottom as a guide line to keep checkerboard straight, or use overhead projector pen to draw line ½ inch from bottom of glass.) Let paint dry 1 hour between coats.

8. Let paint cure 24 hours. Follow paint manufacturer's instructions for a dishwasher-safe finish.

Patterns are 100%

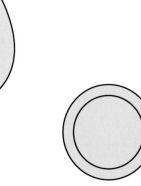

BIRCH ✤ BARK CANDLESTICKS

The rustic splendor of these candlesticks will look lovely in any decor. And, what is even better, anyone can make them for their home!

What You'll Need

White birch logs, approximately 3 inches in diameter

Safety goggles and work gloves

Crosscut hand saw

Sandpaper

Ruler

Marking pen

A ⅜-inch variable-speed drill with a ¾-inch bit

1. Always use safety glasses or goggles when working with wood to shield your face and eyes from flying wood chips and sawdust. Using hand saw, cut three 3-inch-diameter branches, 2½ to 8 inches high.

2. Stand cut logs upright to make certain they stand straight. Use sandpaper if necessary to smooth top and bottom ends.

3. Mark center of log with ruler and pen.

4. Using drill and ¾-inch bit, drill a hole on center mark, approximately 1 inch deep. **Note:** Never leave burning candles unattended.

GOING ✤ BUGGY ✤ NOTECARDS
AND ✤ GARDEN ✤ JOURNAL

Record your gardening successes and boast about them to your family and friends with these charming notecards and journal!

What You'll Need

Cream cardstock for notecards and top of journal

Rubber stamps: dragonfly, ladybug, bumblebee, floral leaf, wiggle

Pigment brush pads: heliotrope, yellow, red, fresh green, lime, cyan

Sticky notes

Scissors

1. Fold cardstock in half to form notecard. Apply heliotrope to dragonfly stamp by pressing pad along rubber surface. Make desired number of prints, reinking after each one. Repeat with bumblebee and ladybug stamps using yellow and red brush pads.

2. To create masks, print 2 of each bug on sticky notes as close as possible to sticky edge. Cut bugs out following lines as closely as possible.

3. Cover bugs along one long side of card with corresponding masks. Apply cyan ink to wiggle stamp. Center stamp along edge and print over any masked bugs that are in that area. Remove masks to reuse on opposite edge. Repeat step. Make a mask for wiggle stamp.

4. Starting in a corner, cover wiggle and bugs with masks. Coat leaf stamp with fresh green ink. Stamp leaves randomly over entire card, moving masks as necessary. Stamp several leaves on sticky notes; cut out.

5. Again starting in a corner, cover wiggle, leaves, and bugs with masks. Coat leaf stamp with lime ink. Stamp leaves randomly over entire card, moving masks as necessary.

6. Write "Garden Journal" on a piece of paper for book cover.

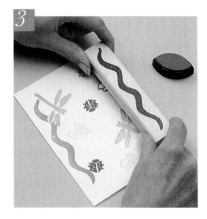

COVERING A BOOK

What You'll Need

Journal

Decorative paper

Ruler

Pencil

White craft glue

Craft stick

Sharp craft knife

1. Measure and cut paper ¾ inches larger than spread-out book. Draw a line ¾ inches from the side and bottom of one side of the book.

2. Brush glue on back of book. Align back of closed book with ¾-inch lines on bottom and side of paper. Press book down. Turn book over and use craft stick to smooth wrinkles. Press paper firmly onto book.

3. Brush a thick layer of glue into crease and spine edge of

book. Gently push paper into crease and onto spine. Use craft stick on spine to smooth out paper. Turn book to front and brush a thin layer of glue into crease and onto front of book. Press paper into crease and onto front of book. Use craft stick as before to adhere paper.

4. Make a cut on each side of spine from edge of paper to edge of book. Cut across, leaving ¼-inch flap. Fold edges in from each side on flap, making a triangle. Put glue on flap and tuck in spine recess. Use craft stick to press down firmly.

5. Open book and place ruler diagonally ¹⁄₁₆ inch away from inside corner edge of book. Cut on diagonal and remove small triangular piece. Repeat on remaining corners. Brush a thin layer of glue on each flap and fold edges over, pushing mitered corners together. Use craft stick as before.

6. Measure and cut 2 pieces of the same or contrasting paper to fit inside front and back covers. Brush with thin layer of glue. Center an end on inside front of book. Press down and use craft stick as before. Repeat with back cover.

BROWN ✦ PAPER
PLANT ✦ WRAPS

For an unusual centerpiece, or to make as hostess gifts, these plant wraps will be the hit of any party!

What You'll Need

Brown paper

Scissors

Pinking shears

Plastic storage bags

Pencil

Ruler

Thread: green, red, yellow, orange, peacock blue, white

Sewing machine

Red felt-tip marker

Glue stick

½ to 1 yard for each wrap: jute, dyed jute, raffia, ribbon, or fancy cord

MACHINE SEWING ON PAPER:

Sewing machines are designed to sew on fabric—not paper. Some irregularities are to be expected in your finished product.

Accept that a small number of skipped stitches will happen. If it happens a lot, re-

place the needle. A needle that is dull or has a burr on the tip can cause skipped stitches. Also, sewing on paper can fray thread— rethread your machine at the first sign of fray.

A needle makes a permanent hole in paper. Learn to stop and start with precision. It is helpful to let up on the pedal and hand crank the last few stitches to a critical stopping point.

Paper can tear easily. If your machine jams thread, don't tug. Cut away all threads in order not to leave a hole in your work.

Do not set your stitch length too close when making a satin stitch on paper: Needle holes too close together will make a perforated line and tear. (Repairs and/or reinforcements can be made on the back side of your work using tape or a paper patch.)

To end, pull all threads to back of paper. Glue first, then snip ends short. Any

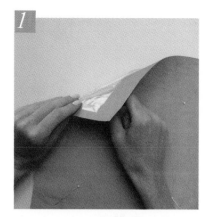

threads left on front can also be glued and snipped. Never backstitch on paper!

Don't worry too much about what will happen to a fancy stitch when you turn a corner. Just sew on the line and try to pivot when the needle is on the right side.

When you pivot on a corner, make the turn with the needle in the paper. The needle should be on its way up.

1. Cut an 11-inch square of brown paper for each plant wrap. Pin a plastic bag to back of paper. Draw guidelines ½ inch apart from each edge inward. Make 3 more guidelines ½ inch from the previous guideline.

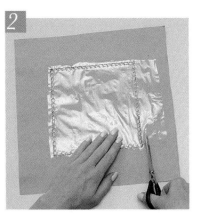  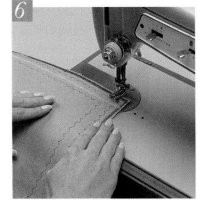

2. Innermost line is always stitched first, securing plastic. Turn paper over and cut off excess plastic. Though not completely waterproof, this plastic liner will prevent a damp flowerpot from spoiling your wrap.

3. Green wrap: Cut out along edges using pinking shears. Use widest satin stitch setting and sew satin stitch on first 2 guidelines. Sew a straight stitch on next 2 guidelines. Sew a curvy line between 2 straight rows. Pull thread ends through to back; glue and trim.

4. Red wrap: Trim with pinking shears. Secure plastic by stitching straight stitch on fourth row. Trim plastic. On first row sew a wavy line; on second row sew a wide satin stitch; on third row sew a wide zigzag or loose satin stitch. Sew just inside fourth row with decorative stitch. Sew a narrow zigzag just inside the pinked edge. Use red marker to color from wavy line to outside edge. Pull thread ends through; glue and trim.

5. Orange wrap: Secure plastic by stitching wavy line on fourth row in orange. Trim plastic. On first row, sew a wide yellow satin stitch; on second row, sew an orange satin stitch (each line begins at paper's edge and ends at other edge). On third row, stitch an orange wavy line. Pull threads through; glue and trim.

6. Blue wrap: Secure plastic by stitching wavy blue line on third row. Trim plastic. As close to the cut edge as you can, stitch a wide blue satin stitch all around. On first row, sew a blue wavy line. On fourth row, sew a wavy line without thread. On second row, sew a white satin stitch (each line begins at paper's edge and ends at other edge). Pull thread ends through; glue and trim.

GAZEBO ❧ BIRDHOUSE

Start your spring with this welcoming gazebo birdhouse. The roof is removable for easy cleaning—generations of birds can visit you year after year!

What You'll Need

Wooden gazebo birdhouse

Acrylic paint: snow white, grey sky, settlers blue, thicket

Brushes: ½-inch flat, #2 flat, 10/0 liner, ⅜-inch angle

Water-base wood sealer or varnish

Matte spray finish

See pages 7–9 of Introduction for instructions on decorative painting.

1. Prepare wood by sanding and using a tack cloth to remove dust. For basecoating only, mix equal parts of paint and water-base varnish. Basecoat following: base, underneath base, roof, eaves, perch, and ball decor on roof top with snow white; outside walls with settlers blue. No other mixing with varnish is necessary. Do not paint inside opening or inside birdhouse;

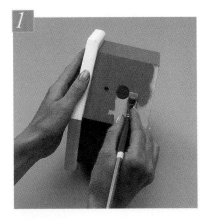

birds will not visit. Let dry and apply each panel of roof and walls by repeating patterns (see pages 119 and 120).

2. Base railing and trim work with snow white. Let dry. This may take 2 or more coats of paint for total coverage. Apply detail pattern to railings. Line all board separation or connections and roof shingles with grey sky. Let dry. Float all connections on railings and underneath each row of shingles with grey sky.

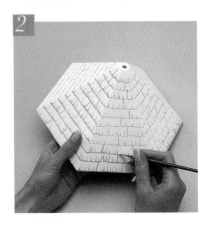

3. Apply detail pattern for ivy. Base leaves with thicket. Replace ball decor.

4. Spray with matte spray finish. Glue roof to body for an indoor birdhouse, or attach a small craft hinge for outdoor use.

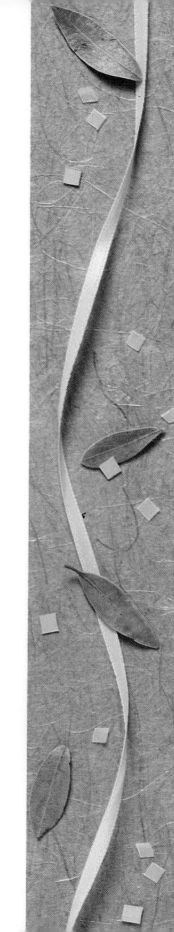

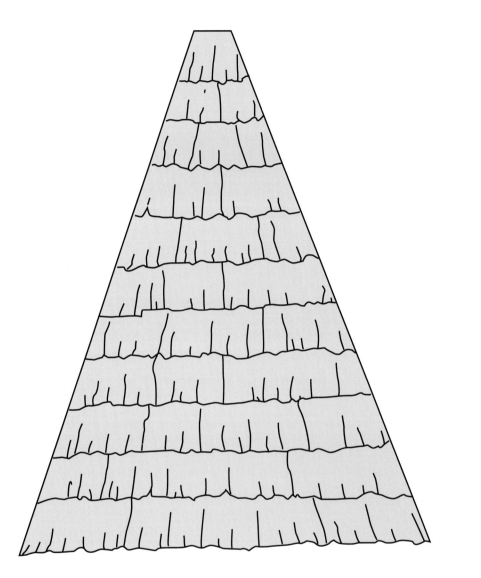

Pattern is 100%

GARDEN ✿ LANTERNS

GARDEN PARTY

121

Create a fairyland that will enchant your party-going guests! These delightful lanterns are fun and can become a family project.

What You'll Need

Cream parchment paper

Cardboard

Pencil

Scissors

Pinking shears

SumiBrush pen (available at art stores)

Art markers: grass green, true green, Spanish orange, hot pink, process red, limepeel green, chartreuse

Soft eraser

Craft glue

Strand white mini-lights

Small vinyl-covered paper clips

1. Trace pattern onto cardboard and cut out. Trace around template (see page 125) to make the number of shades you'd like to create. Three patterns will fit on an 8½×11-inch sheet of parchment.

2. Cut out all shades, using pinking shears for 2 short sides and long side without circular opening. Use plain scissors to cut remaining long side, carefully cutting out circle. Cut about 7 short (about ¹⁄₁₆ inch) notches around circle.

3. Transfer a design (see pages 124 and 125) to each side of a shade. (You can use transfer paper or use a #2 pencil and lightly color across design on wrong side. Then place design and trace onto shade.) Pull shade into final round shape and check to see that design is positioned well. Make any adjustments and proceed to transfer remaining designs.

4. Before using the SumiBrush pen, practice with the thick and thin line. Try to keep your lines loose and relaxed. Outline all designs on shades. Gently erase any carbon or pencil marks.

5. Begin using thick end of art markers to fill in designs. Again, be loose. Don't follow outlines too closely. Allow color to go outside lines or well within them, sometimes allowing parchment to show through. Color each as follows: make leaves grass green and true green; color flowers Spanish orange, hot pink, process red, and limepeel green; color butterflies Spanish orange, process red, chartreuse, and true green; color watering cans process red, Spanish orange, chartreuse, hot pink, and limepeel green.

6. Apply narrow strip of glue to side B only. Do one shade at a time as glue dries

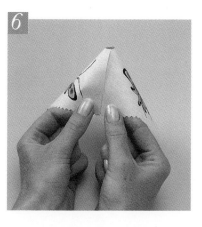

quickly. Carefully bend shade into curve. Position side A over side B about ¼ inch. When sides are positioned, press together and smooth seam. Repeat for all shades.

7. Turn shade upside-down. Take a strand of mini-lights and, just beneath a light,

pinch cord together. Carefully push light through hole until enough cord is exposed on inside of shade so you will be able to thread a paper clip through a strand of cord. Take care not to damage opening of shade.

Patterns are 100%

8. Gently pull open paper clip so it is spread into a *V*. Thread clip onto cord.

9. Settle bulb and clip back into neck of shade, which should be loose but not able to fall off. If necessary, a stitch can be made with needle and embroidery floss to tighten shade opening around base of light. Attach remainder of shades in same manner. Handle shades carefully to prevent dents and creases.

Pattern is 100%

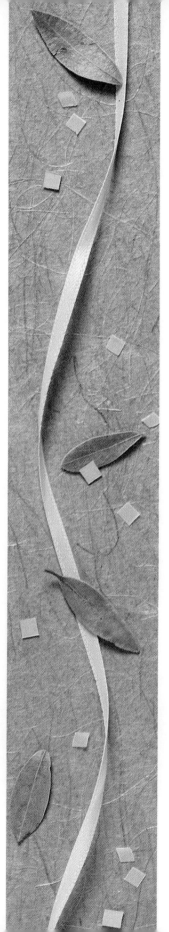

at home in the garden

To dig and delve in nice clean dirt

can do a mortal little hurt.

— *John Kendrick Bangs*

CHARMING ✤ PICTURE ✤ FRAME

Add some romance and elegance to a plain brass frame. Glue on a few charms to make the perfect spot for your special photo!

What You'll Need

4×6-inch brass picture frame

4 corner brass filigrees and filigrees to fill in remaining space on frame

Brass charms: locket, frame and frame back, assorted birds, flowers, hat, etc. (enough to cover frame)

Rubbing alcohol

Waxed paper

Glossy spray varnish

Flower pictures to fit charm frame and locket

Glue stick

Pliers

Disposable plate

Industrial strength adhesive

Toothpicks

1. Clean charms with rubbing alcohol. Working in a well-ventilated area, lay charms on waxed paper and spray with varnish. Let dry.

2. Cut picture to fit charm frame. Using glue stick, adhere picture to frame back. Insert picture into frame. Use pliers to bend prongs over frame back, securing picture in frame. Cut photograph to fit locket. Insert.

3. Arrange filigrees on frame. Working in a well-ventilated area, squeeze adhesive onto a plate and use toothpick to apply to backs of filigrees and onto areas of the frame where they will be placed. Adhere filigrees to frame.

4. Arrange charms, locket, and charm frame on top of filigrees. Adhere one charm at a time by applying adhesive to back of charm and to desired area of frame. Set charm in place. Repeat until all charms are glued on. Let frame lay flat for 24 hours.

Create a family heirloom— generations will enjoy this quilted work of art.

What You'll Need

Template plastic

Utility scissors

Fabric scissors

Ruler

Iron and ironing board

Material: ⅛ yard or scraps of 18 different lights, mediums, and darks for birdhouses and background blocks

9 scraps at least 2-inch square for birdhouse holes using variations of the same color tones

9 scraps at least 8×2½ inches for appliquéd roofs using variations of the same color tones

⅛ yard tan print for inner border

¾ yard blue plaid for outer border

⅛ yard of tan/blue/red print for leaves

⅛ yard dark red solid or print for berries

⅛ yard each of gold, red, and tan/blue plaid for birds

¾ yard of tan/blue stripe for vine

⅓ yard dark red solid or print for binding

1½ yards backing material

1 package low-loft batting, 45×60 inches

Thread: neutral color for piecing blocks and colors to match appliqué pieces.

Quilt Dimensions: 32×50 inches

All pattern pieces and measurements need to have ¼-inch seam allowance added. The lines given in the patterns are sewing lines, not cutting lines, unless otherwise indicated.

For general quilting instructions, see pages 17–21 in the Introduction.

1. To make birdhouse block templates (pattern pieces A through H on page 134): Place template plastic over pattern and trace pattern piece outline. Using a ruler, mark ¼-inch seam allowance around outer edge of pattern piece on plastic. Cut out along inner edge of outside line.

2. To make appliqué templates (pattern pieces I, J, bird, leaf, and berry on page 134): Make the appliqué templates the size that you want the figure to appear on quilt. The seam allowances are added on the material. Cut out along inner edge of outside line.

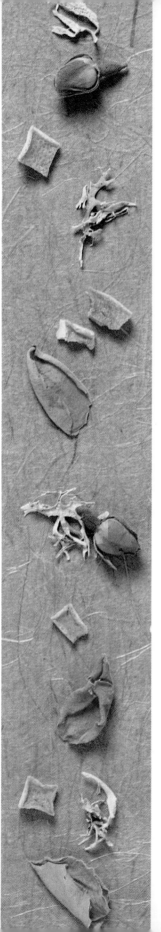

3. For each birdhouse block: pieces A, B, E, G, and H should be cut out of the same material. Pieces C and F should be cut out of the same material. Pieces H and J are both different materials. (For each block, there will be 4 different materials used.) Using templates, mark pieces A, B, D, E, G, and H onto right side of background material using a sharp pencil. Using fabric scissors, cut out pieces. Using templates, mark pieces C and F on right side of birdhouse material. Using fabric scissors, cut out pieces.

4. Piece block in the following sequence (following pattern layout): Sew pieces B and D to C. Sew A to top of piece BDC. Sew pieces E and G to piece F. Sew piece ABCD to piece EFG. Sew piece H to side to complete block. Make 9 blocks.

5. To mark birdhouse appliqué pieces (I and J), place template on right side of fabric. Draw around template

using a sharp pencil. Cut out piece J (birdhouse hole) from 2-inch squares, adding ¼-inch seam allowance. To make a circle, cut out paper the exact size of the circle. Sew a running stitch slightly in from the edge of the fabric starting with a knotted end. Lay the paper piece in the center of the material and pull the loose end of thread around paper—snug but not too tight. Secure with a backstitch. Appliqué piece in place with thread that matches appliqué; turn work over and snip fabric behind circle. Pull out paper with tweezers.

6. Mark and cut piece I. Press seam allowance under and appliqué in place.

7. Sew birdhouse blocks into 3 rows with 3 houses in each row. Sew rows together to make quilt top.

8. For borders: From tan, cut two 1½×36-inch strips and two 1½×20-inch strips. Sew

36-inch strips to sides of quilt top. Sew 20-inch strips to top and bottom of quilt top. From blue plaid, cut two 6½×20-inch strips and two 6½×50-inch strips. Sew 20-inch strips to top and bottom of quilt. Sew 50-inch strips to sides of quilt.

9. To make bias binding: Cut a 21-inch square from tan and blue stripe material. Cut square in half diagonally, making 2 triangles. With right sides facing, sew triangles together (see illustrations on page 133). Mark cutting lines 1 inch apart parallel to long bias edges. Cut into strips. To join strips, lay them perpendicular to each other with right sides facing. Stitch across strips, making a diagonal seam. Using hot steam iron, press under ¼ inch on each side of binding, leaving a ½-inch finished bias binding strip approximately 362 inches long.

10. From bias length, cut six 3½-inch bird perches for

sides, two 10½-inch bird perches for top and bottom, and fourteen 4-inch berry stems.

11. Using finished photo as a guide, sew bias strips to outer border of quilt.

12. Using appliqué templates, mark 2 birds and 1 reverse bird (turn template over before marking) on right side of red material. Adding ¼-inch seam allowance, cut out. Mark and cut 1 bird and 3 reverse birds from tan/blue plaid, 2 birds and 1 reverse bird from gold material, 24 leaves from tan/blue/red print, and 95 berries from dark red solid or print.

13. Press seam allowances under and, using finished photo as a guide, place and sew birds, leaves, and berries to quilt.

14. Cut batting and backing fabric larger than quilt top. Lay backing fabric face down, lay batting on top, and quilt top face up. Baste layers together. Hand or machine quilt layers together. Trim batting and backing.

15. Cut binding fabric into 1½-inch strips (seam allowances are included) and join strips to create one very long strip that is at least 168 inches long. Sew binding fabric to quilt top and turn binding to back of quilt and hand stitch in place.

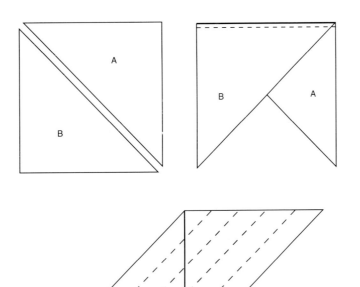

Enlarge patterns 200%

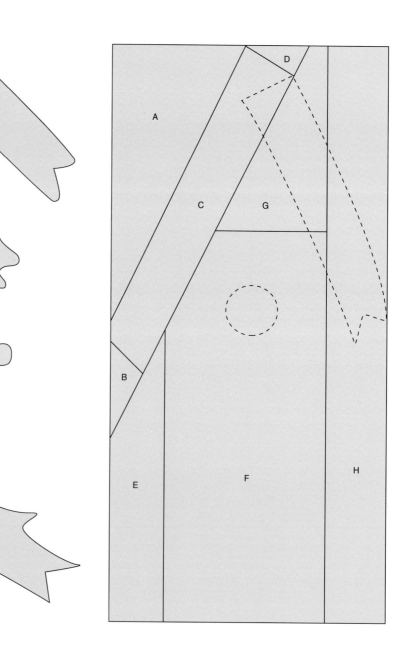

PICKET ❦ FENCE ❦ SHELF

Now you can have your own white picket fence— even if you live in an apartment. This shelf is the perfect place to display your prize posies!

What You'll Need

2 sections redwood border fencing, 36 inches long

³/₄-inch pine board, 6×32 inches

Safety goggles and work gloves

Crosscut handsaw

Marking pencil

Ruler

2¹/₂-inch Phillips-head drywall screws

Heavy-duty staples, staple gun

³/₈-inch variable-speed drill and bit to accommodate the Phillips-head screws (or a Phillips-head screwdriver)

Carpenter's wood filler, spatula

Sandpaper

White latex satin (or semi-gloss) enamel paint

Paintbrush

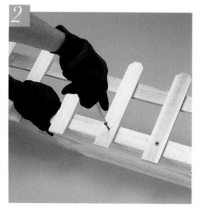

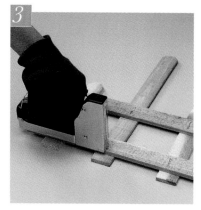

1. Place a section of border fencing on a clean, level work surface. Using crosscut handsaw, cut off long pickets even with shorter pickets (pickets intended to be inserted in ground). This is the front shelf border.

2. Using electric drill or handheld screwdriver and 2¹/₂-inch drywall screws, attach front shelf border, pickets pointing up, to ³/₄-inch pine board along lower rail.

3. For back shelf border: Carefully remove 2 tall ground-stake pickets. Cut pointed bottom edges straight so that all bottom pickets are squared-off. Reposition tall pickets, making sure bottom edges are even with attached pickets. Attach tall pickets to fence brace from back, using staples.

4. Using ruler, mark a point 3 inches down from 2 tall pickets. Drill a counter-sunk hole at this location, to be used to attach shelf to wall.

5. Lay attached fencing face down on work surface. Attach back section to shelf in same manner as front shelf.

6. Fill in front drywall screws with wood filler, according to package directions. Allow to dry and sand lightly if necessary.

7. Paint shelf white. Allow to dry overnight. Using drywall screws, attach to wall.

T i p

Leave the shelf unpainted for a more rustic look, or personalize it to match the color theme of your garden.

BRICK ✦ DOORSTOP

Welcome everyone into your room with this adorable doorstop made from a simple brick. The flower shop look is sure to be a hit!

What You'll Need

Brick

Tracing paper

Transfer paper

Pencil

Acrylic paint: buttermilk, red iron oxide, teal green, sable brown, ebony black, thicket, lemon yellow, pumpkin

Brushes: ½-inch flat, #2 flat, ⅜-inch angle, 10/0 liner

Matte finishing spray

For information on decorative painting, see pages 7–9 of the Introduction.

1. Wash brick with water. Let dry. Basecoat entire brick with buttermilk. Let dry. (If brick has a lot of texture, the drying time will increase.)

2. Apply color change pattern (see page 141). Base roof, flower pot, and flower boxes with red iron oxide. Base door, shutters, and window frames with teal green. Base tree trunk with sable brown. Let dry.

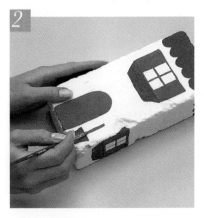

3. Apply detail pattern (shingles, shutter lines, door dimension, flower pot, bricks, and leaf placement). Float and line shingles, shutters, tree trunk, door, flower boxes, and flower pot with ebony black. Also with ebony black, dot doorknob using wooden end of paintbrush. Wash rooftop with water-diluted ebony black.

4. Using a wash of red iron oxide, apply faded bricks. Let dry. Using thicket and #2 flat, apply leaves to flower boxes and tree.

5. Dot flowers on tree and in flower boxes with lemon yellow and pumpkin using end of the brush.

6. Line "WELCOME" with ebony black. Let dry. Finish with complete spray of matte finishing spray.

Tip

Paint a village of brick houses for a border edging a small garden plot. The spray finish will protect your houses from the elements.

Enlarge pattern 135%

DESIGNER ✦ SWEATSHIRT

AT HOME IN THE GARDEN

1 4 2

Turn a plain sweatshirt into a designer gardening shirt with a few snips of the scissors, a panel of border fabric, and a needle and thread.

What You'll Need

Ivory sweatshirt

Scissors

Ruler

Disappearing-ink pen

$5/8$ yard border fabric for medium sweatshirt

$5/8$ yard light fusible webbing

Iron

Sewing machine

Coordinating thread

$3/8$ yard fabric with flower chain for trim

$1/8$ yard ultra hold fusible webbing

Tapestry needle

Embroidery thread

1. Remove waistband from sweatshirt, cutting just above seam line. Lay sweatshirt flat, smoothing out wrinkles.

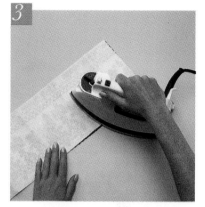

2. Using disappearing ink pen, mark side seams and draw a line across sweatshirt front approximately 2 inches from bottom from side to side. This is the fabric placement guideline. Measure line drawn.

3. Before cutting border material, use above measurement and add $1/2$ inch to both sides to allow for turning edges under, also add $1/2$ inch to top and bottom of desired fabric panel. Press all edges under $1/2$ inch. Iron panel to light fusible webbing, remove paper backing.

4. Position bonded fabric panel using guideline. Press in place. Topstitch as close to fabric edge as possible on all sides.

5. Cut cuffs from sweatshirt; shorten sleeves to desired length. Using disappearing-ink pen, draw straight lines around sleeves 2 to 3 inches from bottom of sleeves. Measure length of line drawn and add 2 inches.

6. Using above measurement, cut 2 lengths from desired fabric adding $1/2$ inch to top and bottom of panel for turning edges under before

cutting. Press under ½ inch along top and bottom edges (long sides), and one short side. Iron each panel to light fusible webbing. Remove paper backing.

7. Beginning with unfolded edge on underarm side of sleeve, pin sleeve panels in place following guideline. Overlap folded edge onto un-folded edge. Fuse panels in place leaving overlapping edges for last in case fabric shifts. Topstitch as close to edges as possible, including folded edges.

8. Cut neck ribbing from sweatshirt.

9. Cut a section of flowers from second fabric (fabric pictured measures approxi-mately 13 inches). Fuse fabric section to ultra hold fusible webbing following manufac-turer's directions. With sharp scissors cut away excess fab-ric. Remove paper backing carefully.

10. Lay flowers approxi-mately 1½ inches from cut neck edge, centering middle flower to center front of shirt. Ease flowers to follow curved line of neck edge; fuse in place.

11. Finish all cut edges, using zigzag or overcast ma-chine stitching.

12. Turn edges under ¼ inch. Hem using embroi-dery floss and buttonhole stitch.

WHERE · LOVEBIRDS · MEET

Invite all types of birds into your yard with this great feeder. This functional bird feeder will be the envy of your neighbors.

What You'll Need

Wood bird feeder

Tracing paper

Transfer paper

Pencil

Wood sealer

Acrylic paint: country red, snow white, sky grey, ebony black, dark chocolate, mink tan, neutral grey, sweetheart pink, raspberry sherbet, harvest gold, denim blue, blue heaven

Brushes: ½-inch flat, #2 flat, ⅜-inch angle, 10/0 liner

½-inch cellophane tape

Matte finishing spray

See wood preparation steps and decorative painting instructions on pages 7–9 of the Introduction.

With basecoating in Step 1, add 1 part wood sealer to 3 parts paint. This adds your first coat of color along with sealing wood.

1. Basecoat roof and eaves with country red; side walls (inside and out), sides, and underneath bottom tray with sky grey; and top inside of tray with snow white. Let dry. Apply side patterns (see page 149). Pattern is repeated on both sides.

2. Base birds, tablecloth, sundae glass, straws, and ice cream with snow white. This will give brighter base colors. Let dry. Base stool and table legs with neutral grey. Apply detail pattern for the bird, sundae, and tablecloth plaid.

3. Base cherry, heart, and stool seats with country red. Base top scoop of ice cream with sweetheart pink, and second scoop with mink tan. Base bird back, tail, wing, and top of head with blue heaven. Base beak and feet with harvest gold.

4. Float the white/blue separation area with blue heaven so it is blended. Float top of heart, top of bird cheeks, and front edge of stool seat with sweetheart pink. Float pink ice cream with raspberry sherbet. Float chocolate ice cream with dark chocolate. Float sundae glass with grey sky. Float blue on birds' tails, wings, behind cheeks, across top of heads, and on backs with denim blue. Float a shade on stool seats, bottom of each twist on table and stool legs, floor line, and stem area of cherry with diluted ebony black. Float a highlight on the twists with grey sky. Float beak and feet with dark chocolate. Line straw stripes with country red.

5. Erase tablecloth pattern lines enough so they are just visible. Dilute country red and apply one direction of tablecloth lines and let dry. Apply opposite direction of lines with diluted country red.

This will create the plaid effect. If necessary, apply another coat of red on small overlapping squares to deepen color. Let dry. Float shade on tablecloth with diluted ebony black.

6. For feed tray: Securely apply ½-inch stripes of tape spaced equally across one direction. (Make sure tape edges are secure to prevent bleeding under tape. Should bleeding occur, when paint is dry touch up with snow white.) Using diluted country red, base stripes and let dry completely. Remove tape, and apply new tape in opposite direction. (This should be placed at right angles to the first stripes.) Base stripes with diluted country red and let dry. Remove tape.

7. Line entire pattern including "LOVE BIRD CAFE" with ebony black. Keep paint the consistency of ink for smoother, thinner lines.

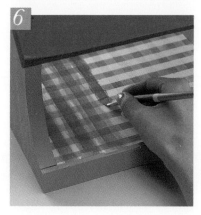

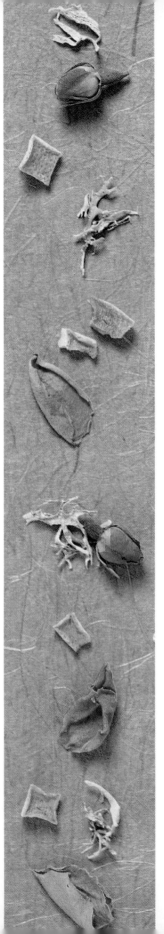

8. Apply roof pattern (pattern is repeated). Line entirely with ebony black and let dry. Float a shade under each shingle with ebony black. Let dry. Spray feeder with matte finishing spray to seal.

Enlarge pattern 125%

WHERE LOVEBIRDS MEET

LOVE BIRD CAFE

Enlarge pattern 125%

AT HOME IN THE GARDEN

149

SUMMER ⟡ GARDEN POTPOURRI

> *"What is that wonderful smell?"* Potpourri brings the garden scent of summer's bouquet into your home.

What You'll Need

¹⁄₈ cup orris (Fx)

¹⁄₃ cup vetiver (Fx)

¹⁄₂ cup oak moss (Fx)

1 teaspoon whole cloves (S)

¹⁄₂ teaspoon ground cinnamon (S)

3 drops lime oil

3 drops orange oil

9 drops Summer Garden oil

1 cup each dried yellow and pink rose petals

1 cup Vva Ursi leaves

¹⁄₂ cup bay leaves

¹⁄₄ cup dried orange peel

¹⁄₃ cup purple larkspur

1 tablespoon lavender seeds

3 to 4 pressed assorted flowers

3 to 4 whole dried assorted roses

Large nonporous bowl

Measuring cup

Measuring spoons

Airtight container or plastic storage bag

Fx = Fixative   S = Spice

1. Mix all spices and fixatives in bowl. Add oils. Rub mixture with your fingers to fix.

2. Add remaining ingredients into bowl. Mix together thoroughly for even distribution.

3. Place mixture in an airtight container and leave for 4 to 6 weeks in a dark place to cure. Rotate mixture every few days to blend and distribute ingredients well.

4. Transfer potpourri to a decorative container and add whole dried roses and pressed garden flowers to decorate.

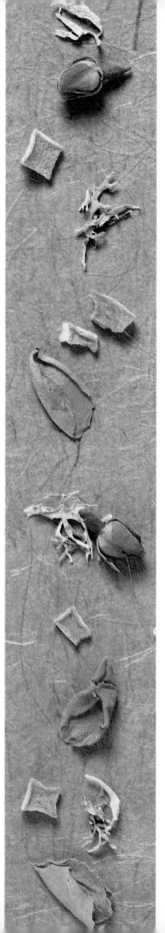

Tips

You can use food storage plastic seal bags for curing your potpourri. When fragrance has diminished you can revitalize by placing the potpourri back into a storage bag and adding a few drops of essential oils to some cotton balls, place inside and seal up. Leave cotton balls in bag for 2 to 3 days and then remove. Fragrance will be restored.

Potpourri Terminology

Potpourri is a fragrant mix of flowers, herbs, spices, leaves, seeds, fixatives, and essential oils that, when blended, create distinct fragrances.

There are five basic groups of ingredients in potpourri: flowers, spices, herbs, fixatives, and essential oils.

FLOWERS are the most important group because of the scent and for decorative purposes. Flowers, flower petals and buds, wood, bark, or fruit peels are used extensively in potpourri blends. These materials will set the theme of your potpourri.

HERBS add a subtle background fragrance. Lavender is the most important and most frequently used in potpourri blends. Others, such as rosemary, lemon mint, bay leaf, and bergamot, are also widely used. These earthy fragrances add interest to the mix, giving it a quality of complexity.

SPICES give potpourri its warmth and sweet smell. They add richness and character to the entire blend of the bouquet. Important spices commonly used are cinnamon, whole cloves, and nutmeg.

FIXATIVES hold or fix and absorb the scents of all the other ingredients; often they contribute their own individual fragrance as well. The most commonly used are orris root (powder or pieces), gum benzoin, chopped corn cob, and oak moss.

ESSENTIAL OILS can dictate the aroma or perfume of a potpourri entirely or can contribute to it, depending on how much you add to the mixture of botanicals. It is better to blend your oil combinations on a piece of thick paper first to develop new fragrances. Don't make mistakes on your plant materials.

RIBBON · TRELLIS · FRAME

Bring an ivy trellis into your home and, unlike your outdoor ivy, it will last all year long.

What You'll Need

2 to 3 sprigs silk ivy

Two 8×10-inch mats with 5×7-inch opening, any color

Pencil

Ruler

Craft knife

Straightedge

Black permanent felt-tip marker

8×10-inch ready-made velvet frameback with stand

12×14-inch square low-loft batting

Craft glue

Craft stick 12×14-inch square natural evenweave linen

Iron

Masking tape

Scissors

5 yards ecru ribbon, ¼ inch wide

Tracing paper

Transfer paper

Tracing wheel

Straight pins with ball tips

Ecru embroidery floss

Embroidery needle

1 yard hook and loop tape

Velcro hook and loop tape

1. Most silk is made up of 2-leaf sections that plug onto a stem. Cut stem and pull off ivy sections. You will only use the small and medium leaves.

2. Take one mat and enlarge 5×7-inch opening: (Measure ¼ inch in from the inside opening and mark a line all around with a pencil. Lay a straightedge on the line and cut away excess with a sharp craft knife. Blacken the outside edge (this mat only) with a felt-tip marker. Align this mat with frameback (wrong side) and trace a pencil line onto frameback around mat's inside opening. Put both pieces aside.

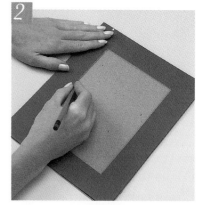

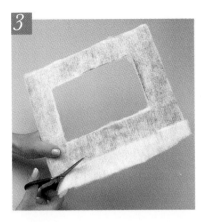

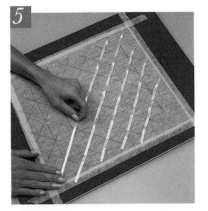

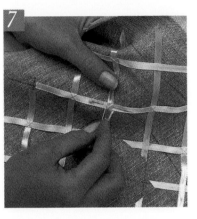

5. Carefully pin ribbon along diagonal guidelines in one direction. Allow ribbon to extend about 1½ inches beyond borders of mat at inside and outside edges.

6. Next, pin ribbon in other diagonal direction, weaving over and under intersecting ribbons. You will have to adjust pins to allow ribbon to weave. Pin at each intersection. Untape work and remove from work surface.

3. Take second mat and glue on batting. (Rub a thin coating of glue on mat; press batting on glue and let dry briefly). Trim batting even with mat edges. Put aside.

4. Press wrinkles out of linen using iron. Tape linen on tabletop or cardboard using masking tape. Tape along edges, keeping fabric taut and straight. Transfer design to linen using tracing wheel. Leave work taped down until Step 7.

7. Thread needle with an 18-inch length of floss (3-ply) and embroider an *X* at every intersection to hold ribbon in place. Remove pins as you go. Secure each *X* at back with

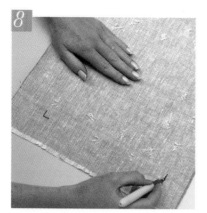

9. Take mat with batting and lightly spread a little glue on batting. Place linen face down on a clean work surface, and center mat on linen, batting side down, aligning at corners. Cut an *X* in the center, stopping ¼ inch from corners. Cut away all but 1 inch from linen.

10. To stretch linen over mat: Fold corners over first and glue in place. Next fold and glue sides, keeping as flat as possible. Trim excess fabric where needed. Let dry.

11. Take mat with black edging and spread glue over one side. Align this mat with the linen-covered mat and glue together. Press under a heavy book and allow to dry for 1 to 2 hours.

tiny stitches. (This *X* stitch is the standard cross-stitch).

8. Lightly glue down any loose ribbon ends along inside and outside edges and let dry 10 minutes. Trim to within 1 inch from edge of

pattern. (Do not trim inside mat opening yet). Transfer the 4 outer corner positions by putting a straight pin through to the wrong side, and marking each corner on the wrong side with a fabric marker. Remove straight pins.

12. Cut eight 1-inch pieces from hook side of hook and loop tape and stick 1 on each side of each corner.

13. Cut loop side of hook and loop tape to fit around pencil line on back of frame-back. Photo or mirror can be placed in center and is held in place by hook and loop tape edge and mat edge.

14. Position ivy sprigs randomly under ribbon on front of linen. When arrangement is pleasing, use straight pins to pin ivy in place. Hide pins under ribbon. Unruly ivy can be glued lightly in place.

Tip

Make smaller frames to give as gifts with the kids' school pictures—the grandparents will really appreciate the thoughtfulness. And, if grandma's favorite flower is the rose, add those instead of the ivy. Make each frame a personal message of love!

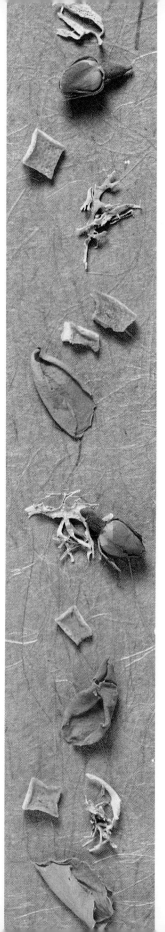

BEADED ♦ BIRDHOUSE
TREASURES

This stunning tree full of birds and birdhouses is a must for the bird-lover in your midst. The beads add polish to the easy-to-do plastic canvas.

What You'll Need

14-count cream plastic canvas

Cream thread

Seed beads (see color chart), 1 package each color

Ceramic birdhouse and bird buttons

Wooden window tree

4 feet cream ribbon, ⅛ inch wide

Small green garland

Hot glue gun, glue sticks

Black embroidery floss

Color	Mill Hill #
Light green	525
Dark green	332
Brown	2023
Gold	0557
Pearl	479
Grey	150
Light yellow	2002
Dark yellow	128
Light blue	2007
Dark blue	020
Pink	62035
Red	165
White	3015
Black	2014

See plastic canvas instructions on pages 13–14 of the Introduction.

When all designs are finished, use a pair of sharp scissors and cut 1 row away from stitches to cut out design.

Wrap garland around limbs of tree and attach each end with a drop of hot glue.

Cut ribbon into twelve 4-inch pieces. Stitch an ornament to center of a ribbon; tie ribbon around limb with a bow. Use a drop of hot glue on each bow to anchor it. Hot glue bird button to top of tree and birdhouse button to base.

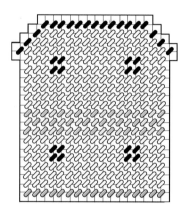

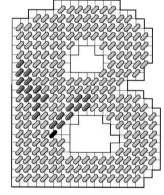

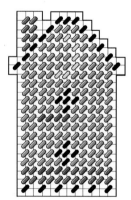

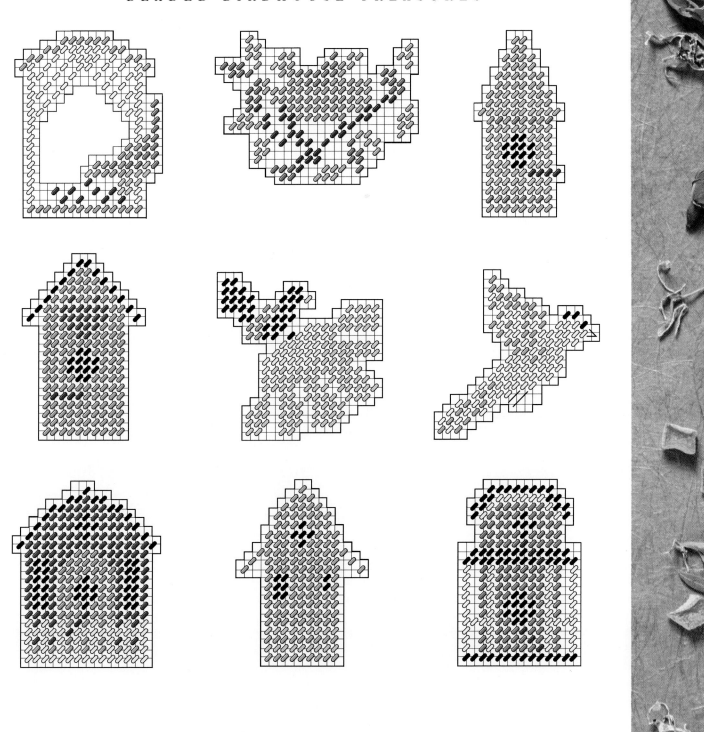

VICTORIAN ❧ GARDEN ❧ PLATE

This robin's egg blue display plate is sure to complement your decor— and if blue isn't your color, choose another to enhance your room.

What You'll Need

Clear glass plate

Ruler

Overhead projector pen

Acrylic enamel paints: true gold metallic, baby blue

Fine-line paint bottle with removable metal tip

Garden theme Victorian decoupage papers

Scissors

Decoupage finish

1-inch sponge brush

Palette

Waxed paper

1. Wash plate. Painting must be done on a clean, oil-free surface.

2. Using ruler and overhead projector pen, make dots every 1½ inches around outside rim of plate. On front of plate rim connect dots by making scalloped lines. Several scallops may need to be adjusted if dots do not come out evenly.

3. Pour metallic gold paint into fine-line bottle. Screw on metal tip. Place plate upside-down on piece of waxed paper. Follow scalloped lines to paint gold lines on back of plate. Paint gold line around inner edge of plate rim and make dots with paint between scallops. Remove metal tip and paint thicker gold line around outside edge of plate rim. (All painting is done on back of plate.) Allow to dry at least an hour. Carefully remove marking lines from front of plate with a damp cloth.

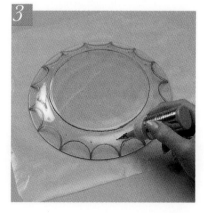

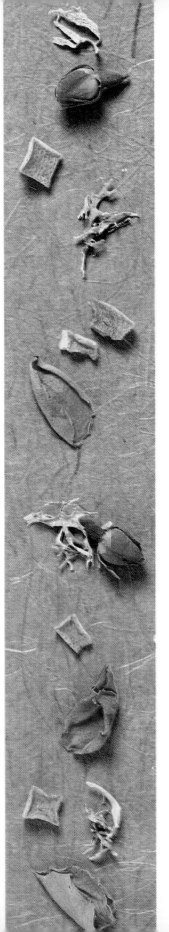

4. Cut out designs from decoupage paper. Arrange cutouts as you wish them to appear on plate.

5. Place cut-outs in position face down on back of plate. Pour some decoupage finish onto palette. Picking up a cut-out at a time, use sponge brush to coat front of paper with decoupage finish. Smooth cut-out face down onto back of plate. Repeat for each cut-out, being sure to smooth out bubbles and edges. Allow to dry before continuing.

6. Using sponge brush, apply thin coat of decoupage finish over entire center portion of plate back. When dry and clear, apply another coat of finish. Allow to dry overnight.

7. Squirt puddle of blue paint onto clean palette. Using sponge brush, paint entire back of plate. When dry (about 1 hour), apply a second coat of paint. It may take several coats to get complete coverage.

FLOWER · GARDEN · BOX

Summer's treasures are intricately executed with garden bunches of dried roses, peonies, and sunflowers divided into geometric patterns and textures.

What You'll Need

3×10×18-inch stained wood shadow box, with 8 pockets

3 blocks dry floral foam, 3×4×8 inches each

Craft knife

Hot glue gun, glue sticks

Sheet moss

22-gauge floral wire

Wire cutters

7 stems dried pink roses

7 stems dried yellow roses

3 stems dried burgundy peonies

4 stems dried sunflowers

9 stems dried lotus pods (assorted sizes)

2 dried pomegranates

1 stem dried hydrangea

1 package dried linum grass

1. Cut and hot glue foam into pockets. Cut wire into 3-inch pieces and shape into *U*-shaped pins.

2. Cover foam lightly with moss around edges, securing with wire pins.

3. Cut dried flowers and insert into pockets in groups. Hot glue if necessary.

4. Cover any exposed foam with moss.

Tips

You can use this same technique on any size shadow box. The texture box can be used as a table arrangement or by applying a picture hanger to the back you can also hang it on the wall. To add spice and fragrance to your texture box, try using cinnamon sticks, garlic bulbs, or bay leaves.

sources for products

Most of the crafts used in the projects in this book, such as brushes, paints, fusible webbing, or tapes, are available at craft, hobby, or fabric stores nationwide. Other products may give equally good results. Specialized products that are specific to a project are listed below by page number; these products are also widely available. For further information, contact the manufacturers at the addresses given at the bottom of the page.

Page 24: Silk flowers, greens, fruits, swag: Wang's International, Inc. Fray Check fabric glue: Prym-Dritz Corp. Gold mesh ribbon: Wright's. **Page 27:** Aida cloth: Charles Craft. Floss and Wildflower Caron Collection floss: The DMC Corp. **Page 36:** Americana acrylic paint (Holly Green, Pumpkin, Baby Pink, Lemon Yellow): DecoArt. Ceramcoat acrylic paint (Blue Heaven): Delta Technical Coatings, Inc. Folk Art acrylic paint (Heather): Plaid Enterprises, Inc. **Page 52:** Silk flowers, greens, gate, wreath: Wang's International, Inc. Fray Check fabric glue: Prym-Dritz Corp. Floral ribbon: Princess Fabrics. Americana acrylic paint: DecoArt. **Page 62:** Silk flowers, greens, fruit, vegetables, wreath: Wang's International, Inc. **Page 65:** Pellon Wonder Under fusible webbing: Freudenberg Nonwovens. Old Fashion cotton quilt batting: Morning Glory Products. **Page 69:** Americana and Ultra Gloss acrylic paints, brush

and hand cleaner, wood sealer: DecoArt. Creatively Yours clear silicone: Loctite Corp. Brush tub, Mixtique brushes, LaCorneille Wash brushes: Loew-Cornell, Inc. Tooling copper: Dick Blick. **Page 78:** Leathercolor paint: The Leather Factory, Inc. Antique gold dimensional paint: Tulip Productions. **Page 81:** Basket: Viking Woodcrafts, Inc. Liquitex Concentrated Artist Colors paints: Binney & Smith, Inc. **Page 87:** Canvas floor mat: Dick Blick. Americana acrylic paints: DecoArt. Mixtique brushes, brush tub: Loew-Cornell, Inc. Speedball Painters Metallic Opaque paint marker: Hunt Manufacturing Company. **Page 94:** Folk Art acrylic paint and textile medium, stencil brushes, wall stencil #26676: Plaid Enterprises, Inc. **Page 98:** Visions Air-Painting System kit (#62986), Visions Acrylic Opaques and Tints, and Ivy Stencils: The Testor Corp. **Page 102:** HeatnBond Lite iron-on adhesive: Therm O Web, Inc. **Page 106:** Ultra Gloss acrylic enamel paint: DecoArt. **Page 111:** Dragonfly, lady bug, bumblebee, floral leaf, wiggle rubber stamps: Hot Potatoes. Color Box Pigment brush pads: Clearsnap Inc. **Page 117:** Birdhouse: Cabin Crafters. Americana acrylic paint (Snow White, Grey Sky): DecoArt. Plaid Folk Art acrylic paint (Settlers Blue, Thicket): Plaid Enterprises, Inc. **Page 121:** Velverette craft glue: Delta Technical Coatings, Inc. Prismacolor art markers: Berol USA. Pigma SumiBrush pen:

Sakura of America. **Page 128:** Brass charms: Creative Beginnings. Spray varnish, Industrial Strength Adhesive glue: Krylon. **Page 138:** Americana acrylic paint (Buttermilk, Red Iron Oxide, Sable Brown, Ebony Black, Teal Green, Lemon Yellow, Pumpkin). Folk Art acrylic paint (Thicket): Plaid Enterprises, Inc. **Page 142:** Lite and Ultra Hold HeatnBond fusible webbing: Therm O Web. Embroidery thread: The DMC Corp. **Page 145:** Wood birdfeeder: Cabin Crafters. Americana acrylic paint (Country Red, Snow White, Sky Grey, Ebony Black, Dark Chocolate, Mink Tan, Neutral Grey). Folk Art acrylic paint (Sweetheart Pink, Raspberry Sherbert, Harvest Gold): Plaid Enterprises, Inc. Ceramcoat acrylic paint (Denim Blue, Blue Heaven): Delta Technical Coatings, Inc. **Page 153:** Embroidery floss: The DMC Corp. Velverette craft glue: Delta Technical Coatings, Inc. **Page 159:** Small wooden tree: Taylors Workshop. Mill Hill beads and buttons: Gay Bowles Sales. Estaz garland: Maderia Marketing LTD. Embroidery floss: The DMC Corp. **Page 162:** Ultra Gloss acrylic enamel paint: DecoArt. Decoupage paper, Royal Coat decoupage finish: Plaid Enterprises, Inc. **Page 165:** Wood texture box: Flowerfields & Co.

Berol USA
Div. of Berol Corp.
Brentwood, TN 37024-2248

Binney & Smith, Inc.
1100 Church Ln.
Easton, PA 18044-0431

Cabin Crafters
1225 W. 1st St.
Nevada, IA 50201

Charles Craft
P.O. Box 1049
Laurinburg, NC 28353

Clearsnap Inc.
Box 98
Anacortes, WA 98221

Creative Beginnings
475 Morro Bay Blvd.
Morro Bay, CA 93442

DecoArt
P.O. Box 360
Stanford, KY 40484

Delta Technical Coatings, Inc.
2550 Pellissier Pl.
Whittier, CA 90601

Dick Blick
P.O. Box 1267
Galesburg, IL 61402-1267

The DMC Corp.
10 Port Kearny
South Kearny, NJ 07032

Flowerfields & Co.
131 Standish
Schaumburg, IL 60193

Freudenberg Nonwovens
Pellon Division
1040 Avenue of the Americas
New York, NY 10018

Gay Bowles Sales
1310 Plainfield Ave.
Janesville, WI

Hot Potatoes
2109 Grantland Ave.
Nashville, TN 37204

Hunt Mfg. Co.
230 S. Broad St.
Philadelphia, PA 19102

The Leather Factory, inc.
P.O. Box 50429
Ft. Worth, TX 76105

Krylon
31500 Solon Rd.
Solon, OH 44139

Loctite Corp.
705 North MOuntain Rd.
Newington, CT 06111

Loew-Cornell, Inc.
563 Chestnut Ave.
Teaneck, NJ 07666-2490

Maderia Marketing LTD
600 E. 9th St., 3rd floor
Michigan City, IN 46360

Morning Glory Products
302 Highland Drive
Taylor, TX 76104

Plaid Enterprises, Inc.
1649 International Blvd.
Norcross, GA 30093

Princess Fabrics
1040 Ave. of America
New York, NY 10018

Prym-Dritz Corp.
Box 5028
Spartanburg, SC 29304

Sakura of America
30780 San Clemente St.
Hayward, CA 94544

Taylors Workshop
114 S. Jayland Ave.
Durham, NC 27703

The Testor Corp.
620 Buckbee St.
Rockford, IL 61104

Therm O Web, Inc.
770 Glenn Ave.
Wheeling, IL 60090

Tulip Productions
A Division of Polymerics, Inc.
24 Prime Park Way
Natick, MA 01760

Viking Woodcrafts, Inc.
1317 8th St. SE
Waseca, MN 56093

Wang's International, Inc.
4250 Shelby Dr.
Memphis, TN 38118

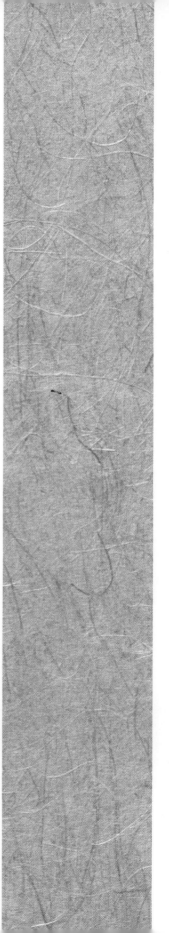

i n d e x